Uniquely His Love, Matilda

Matilda Kipfer

With Pam Eichorn

Uniquely His Love, Matilda
by Matilda Kipfer

Printed in the United States of America

ISBN 1-594670-07-2

Unless otherwise indicated, Bible quotations are taken from The NIV Study Bible (version[s]) of the Bible. Copyright © 1985 by The Zondervan Corporation.

The Holy Bible, The Amplified Version. Copyright © 1987 by Zondervan

Scripture taken from *The Message*, The New Testament, Psalms and Proverbs, Copyright © 1993, 1994, 1995 by Eugene H. Peterson. Used by permission of NavPress Publishing Group.

The Holy Bible, New King James Version, Personal Study Bible. Copyright © 1990, 1995 by Thomas Nelson Inc.

Xulon Press
www.XulonPress.com

Xulon Press books are available in bookstores everywhere, and on the Web at www.XulonPress.com.

Dedication

I dedicate this book to my mother who instilled in me
a hunger for God.

Acknowledgments

Thank-you… to my dear husband, Wallace of 55 years, our four children and their spouses, Galen and Debbie, Carolyn and Dennis, Don and Carol, and Mary Jane and Derek. Our eleven grand children and three great-grand-children. You have made me the richest woman in town! Your love, blessings, and support made it possible for me to keep going.

Thank-you Susan Goodnight, for believing in my ability to write and for helping me to get started in '95. (So I am a little slow)

Thank-you Pam Eichorn (my co-author), her husband and her four children, for graciously sharing your wife and mother. Pam, you have made this journey exciting!!

For all our former pastors Dave and Kathryn Beachy, Dan and Martha Yutzy, and Titus and Barbara Kauffman. Thank-you for being able to help us walk through a very controversial assignment.

I wish to acknowledge Nelson and Ada Litwiller, John and Yovonne Garlington, Wayne and Martha Myers, and the many Aglow Advisers who taught me so much on this journey.

To the host of Intercessors who have been so faithful in praying for us!! Thank you so very much. Heaven will reward you! Words fail to express my deep gratitude for your faithfulness.

Last but not least, I would like to give honor and thanks to my brother Jerry, who kept his hand on my back, encouraging me to reach higher and go deeper in the love of God. Your wise council and encouragement gave me the strength to continue.

Endorsements

Matilda is not only a woman of impeccable character, she is a warm and loving friend. As she shares her life in walking with God, you will be blessed, challenged, and changed.

Sharon Barrett
Managing Director of U.S. Fellowships
Aglow International

Caution: The words in this book will cause Matilda's contagious faith to spread. These ingredients will produce faith, hope, and love in your spirit. But be assured, great fruit will be produced!

Evelyn Steele
Aglow International U.S. Board

Matilda Kipfer is one of the most inspiring, dynamic, and refreshingly honest speakers on "who we are in Christ". As a former pastor of Matilda and her husband Wallace, I have seen them not only speak about the goodness of God, they are living testimonies of God's work through many struggles as well as victories. Matilda is uniquely gifted in teaching God's word with refreshing illustrations of its effectiveness in her life and others. I heartily recommend this book.

Titus Kauffman
Pastor

Matilda Kipfer is one of those incredible women who are, "Uniquely His." Her warm and winsome personality, and her approachability, give those around her easy access to a wealth of spiritual depth within. Her ministry has literally touched lives around the world, impacting them with the love of Jesus which she expresses so beautifully. You will be blessed by what Matilda has to share in this book.

Jane Hansen
President, Aglow International

Contents

Foreword

The article below describes my journey the best of anything I have ever read. It was as though it had been written divinely for me and therefore I will not attempt to even compose anything grandiose or compelling. And for all of you who as you read this book can relate to this journey… in the words of Eugene Peterson's *The Message…*

> "And how blessed all those in whom you live,
> whose lives become roads you travel;
> They wind through lonesome valleys, come upon brooks,
> Discover cool springs and pools brimming with rain!
> God-traveled, these roads curve up the mountain, and
> at the last turn-Zion! God in full view!"

How Do You Think of God?

At first, I saw God as my observer, my judge, keeping track of the things I did wrong, so as to know whether I merited heaven or hell when I die. He was out there sort of like a president. I recognized His picture when I saw it, but I didn't really know Him.

But later on when I met Christ, it seemed as though life were rather like a bike, but it was a tandem bike, and I noticed that Christ was in the back helping me to pedal. I don't know when it was He suggested we change places, but life has not been the same since I took the back seat to Jesus, my Lord. Christ makes life exciting! When I had control, I knew the way. It was rather boring, but predictable. It was the shortest distance between two points.

But when He took the lead, He knew delightful long cuts up mountains, and through rocky places and at breakneck speeds. It was all I could do to hang on! Even though it looked like madness, He said, "Pedal!"

I was worried and anxious and asked, "Where are you taking me?" He laughed and didn't answer and I started to learn to trust. I forgot my boring life and entered into adventure. And when I'd say "I'm scared," He would lean back and touch my hand.

He took me to people with gifts I needed, gifts of healing, acceptance and joy. They gave me their gifts to take on my journey, our journey, my Lord's and mine. And we were off again. He said, "Give the gifts away; they're extra baggage, to much weight." So I did, to the people we met, and I found that in giving, I received, and still our burden was light.

I did not trust Him at first with control of my life. I thought He would wreck it, but He knows bike secrets. He knows how to make it bend to sharp corners, jump to clear high rocks and fly to shorten scary passages. I am learning to shut up and pedal in the strangest places. And I am even beginning to enjoy the view and the cool breeze on my face with my delightful constant companion, Christ.

And when I'm sure I just can't do any more, He just smiles and says. . ."Pedal!"

Author Unknown

CHAPTER 1

Charting the Course

"Ladies and gentlemen; please make sure that your seat belts are securely fastened and your trays and seat backs are in an upright and locked position. Welcome to the friendly skies and have a nice flight."

I find myself quite often viewing the earth from the height of the clouds. The roads and highways look like ribbons with toy cars and trucks threading their way across the country. Somehow the earth doesn't seem so formidable at this distance. Everything is scaled down in size and one has an expanded view of our planet. I think of how small it must look from God's vantage point. David, in Psalm 2, described God sitting in the heavens laughing, as nations, kings and rulers took counsel together against the Lord. "What is man that you are mindful of him, the son of man that you care for him?" (Psalm 8:4).

As a little girl I remember sitting at the kitchen table eating dinner and hearing the sound of a single engine plane. We would all drop our forks and run out into the yard to stare up into the sky as we attempted to locate the sound that was coming from the clouds. The joy and amazement that filled me as I watched the plane fly overhead, still lingers in my memory. It was just unimaginable that this young Mennonite girl born in 1928 at the beginning of the Great Depression, and the youngest of fourteen children, would ever fly. Yet today I have flown over 900,000 miles on United Airlines alone, carrying the Gospel of Jesus Christ.

My parents were John and Fanny Jantzi. My father's family came from Canada and my mother's family came from Ohio. Both my father and my mother were raised in Amish households. Later, both of their families moved to the Fairview, Michigan area, and it was there that my parents met and were married. They later left the Amish church and joined the Mennonite church. They had four children while living in Fairview, then, hearing of land in Au Gres, Michigan, they moved there to homestead.

At the time the land was primitive and had to be cleared by hand. During this time, my mother gave birth to two sets of twins, sixteen months apart. Within the first twenty years of their marriage my parents had fourteen children. There were twenty years between my oldest sibling and myself.

I cannot remember a time that my father did not have health problems. He was diagnosed with severe anemia, but now we wonder if it may have been leukemia. We all had to work hard to survive.

One day one of my brothers said, "Dad and Mom had too many children." I don't believe that he meant any harm but as the youngest, I received that statement as the truth. It became embedded in my heart.

"I couldn't have been wanted."

"I was a mistake."

Such thoughts as these began to dominate my thinking. I didn't like the way I looked and I especially disliked my name. I did not think "Matilda" was a suitable name for a child. Furthermore, I didn't have a middle name and I could not even say my name correctly because of my stuttering.

I really believe that my feelings of rejection started in the womb. My mother instructed us girls about the importance of good thoughts when we became pregnant. Even if the pregnancy was unplanned, we needed to receive this child and love him immediately and completely. Later, after she died, a brother told us that this had been one of her deepest concerns. She felt she may have done the very thing she had cautioned us against because of her dismay over yet another pregnancy. She felt strongly that she had negatively affected some of her children. I realized that I was one of them and that it had pained her deeply.

I was never sure whether my father loved me or not, but I began to be confident of one thing. If I had been a son, I would have had more value. Although we worked side by side in the fields and barn, I could never understand why the girls did not have the same privileges as the boys. They went to town with Dad and could go swimming as we stood on the shore and watched. A feeling began to burn within me: women were God's afterthought and men were superior.

Transferred Feelings

Having this poor relationship with my earthly father affected the way I felt about God. I grew afraid of Him. I would read my Bible, but instead of it becoming a love letter to me from God, it became a document that underscored God's holiness and my sinfulness. I became extremely sin-conscious. A little song we used to sing in Sunday School struck fear in me: "He sees all I do, He hears all I say. My God is writing all the time, time, time!" I felt that He was watching every bad thing that I did. I read my Bible through this distorted filter system. I began to avoid portions of scripture that seemed to reinforce my warped concept of God and His thought concerning women.

Genesis 19:6-8, the story of Lot offering his daughters to the men of Sodom, was one of these scripture. How could Lot sacrifice his own daughters? Were they worth nothing? He gave lusting men permission to defile them in exchange for the safety of the two male visitors! Did Lot have no remorse? This fed the fear that was growing inside of me: women really were inferior, therefore I was inferior.

I appreciate the godly men in my life who believed the Biblical principles of integrity, modesty, and godly submission. Often, however, the principle was lost in the application and confusion was the result. It was through this confusion that I began to view scripture. First Corinthians 11 discusses the woman and her covering. Verse 5 reads, "And every woman who prays or prophesies with her head uncovered dishonors her head—it is just as though her head were shaved."

Verse 13 says, "Judge for yourselves: Is it proper for a woman to pray to God with her head uncovered?" If praying and prophesying was the purpose for the covering, then why was a woman not allowed to pray or prophesy in the church?

I was certain that 1 Peter 3:1 was the text read at every wedding: "Wives, in the same way be submissive to your husbands so that, if any of them do not believe the word, they may be won over without words by the behavior of their wives." I remember thinking that Ephesians 5:25 would have been a much better verse to use: "Husbands, love your wives, just as Christ loved the church and gave himself up for her." A root of bitterness began to rise within me towards God for making me a woman.

When I was eleven, I invited Jesus into my heart and was baptized at the Riverside Mennonite Church. I loved Jesus as my Savior but the Lordship of Jesus Christ was frightening to me. I had read many stories of the Christians during the Reformation who were burned at the stake, drowned in rivers, or had fled for their lives. I read of the missionaries who were eaten by cannibals or died of disease in the jungles of Africa. I was afraid of giving Him my entire life. I did not understand that "my life" meant my past, present, and future. "'For I know the plans I have for you, declares the Lord, plans to prosper you and not to harm you, plans to give you hope and a future'" (Jer. 29:11). It was not until later in life that I understood the safety and security His Lordship would bring.

In our culture verbal affirmation was discouraged in order to prevent prideful thoughts of oneself. This lack of affirmation increased my insecurities, therefore, I became a performer and carried this into my relationship with God. I was a very good student and was always trying to prove that I had as much right to be born as the rest of the children. Even though my grades were excellent, I still did not receive the praise I longed for.

I became jealous of my older brothers and sisters, for they knew a father who sang in the field, led songs in the church, and served as Sunday School Superintendent. The father I knew was often harsh, filled with stress, and very sad. As a young child I was unable to understand this cloud hanging over us.

Major Changes

When I was nine, my father suffered a massive stroke. His health steadily deteriorated and he was no longer able to communicate or provide for his family. His last years were spent lying on the couch or in a wheelchair, unable to talk or feed himself. My mother cared for him for five years. Then, in 1940, when I was fourteen, he died of pneumonia.

Standing by his casket, I realized that I would never really know if my father loved me or wanted me. A wave of loneliness overwhelmed me. Even after his death, the cloud was still there.

The responsibility that was placed on the five children remaining at home was immense. Although I had been a very good student, I had to withdraw from school to work on the farm. The principal came to our home and attempted to persuade my mother to let me remain in school. "You cannot do this to her. Don't you realize the kind of student she is?"

But education was not considered a priority. The real work and need was in the fields. One dreary fall day as we were harvesting beans, I saw the school bus pass by our home. In my heart, I knew the horrible truth. The only chance I had to prove myself, to prove my worth, had just gone by without me. My formal education ended in the eighth grade.

I realize now that the harshness of those deep-seated beliefs about my self-worth and my value were not true. The facts were accurate; I was the fourteenth child and I could not change that. What I could change was my belief that I was not loved. I have come to believe the life-giving truth of God's incredible love for me and for you. Oh, I still realize that I was not planned for, but I know for positive sure that I was not a mistake!!

In spite of what appeared to be missed opportunities and a modest lifestyle, I was blessed with a rich and godly heritage that developed determination, perseverance, and patience in me. These qualities would later be invaluable for the ministry that God had prepared for me.

The older I become, the more I understand that my mother and father walked in the light they had. They lived their Christianity daily and though poverty and illness struck, they did not falter in their faith. Tragedy in one's life and debilitating health problems can attack a person's sense of value and reduce reality to bleak, discouraging levels. As an adult I now appreciate the faith and courage it took for my parents to keep going. Their inner stamina was remarkable.

I am proud to be their daughter and I am happy to tell you that of the twelve children that survived, all have been active in the church. One became an evangelist, one a theologian, and the remaining sons and daughters were either church trustees, deacons, or Sunday school teachers. And I, the unexpected youngest child, have traveled the world, teaching and encouraging women of all denominations and telling them of Jesus Christ's incredible love for them.

Sweet Memories

Yes, even though life seemed harsh, and understanding was not there, certain memories evoke sweetness no matter how uncertain the times may have been. One such sweet memory is of my mother. She had only a third grade education. She never spoke in public or taught Sunday school and she never gave a public testimony, but she was rich in character and compassion. Her keen sense of humor and her unselfishness left its mark on all of us children. In the morning we would find her reading the Bible and praying. Our last recollection at night was of her praying. The translation of the Bible into her daily living was so accurate that even now that she is gone she still speaks to me.

There was a woman in our church whose husband had been unfaithful. She also had an affair and became pregnant. After the baby was born my mother and I went over to visit her. The mother insisted that the child was her husband's but we could clearly see that it was not. I remember that my mother's response was one of restoration and not of condemnation. She walked that woman through the adoption process, the church discipline, and the rejection from the church and her family.

I marvel at my mother's ability to create happy memories. I love Christmas. The little girl in me still likes to celebrate it. We grew up in depression years and there really wasn't money for gifts. On Christmas Eve we would set out a bowl and in the morning there would be an orange, some nuts, and candy in the bowl. What a treat!

It is hard for my children and grandchildren to comprehend the joy a small bowl of candy could bring. I can still remember the peanut shells that were stuck to the hard candy. In spite of this, it was like gold to us.

In our church Christmas trees and decorations were considered worldly so there were none in our home. We were allowed to participate in the school programs though and to decorate the Christmas tree at school. It was so much fun and I thought it was beautiful.

It helps when we share stories from our childhood with our children and grandchildren so they can understand how we think. Even to this day it doesn't take much to make me grateful and I appreciate little things that people do. I don't crave more things and I am sure this comes from a hard life. The depression years molded us and I give my mother credit for the happy memories I have in spite of the poverty around us.

The little girl in me still awakens with the joys of Christmas. I love baking big round cookies with raisins for eyes and mouth, decorating the tree, hanging the garland, and making my house pretty. I asked my daughter, Mary Jane, if she thought I would ever lose this feeling and her reply was, "Never? You have been excited about Christmas ever since you were a little girl."

This year a sadness came over me. Christmas wasn't the same as in other years. We seem to have forgotten the simple joys. The trials of life and the influences from the outside world have robbed us of our contentment with simple celebrations and simple pleasures. In our exuberance we have lavished those we love with excess. I just cannot help longing for my loved ones to have the same happiness and gratitude, which we had for whatever we received.

I loved to hear my mother sing. She had a beautiful voice and she would sing songs of heaven. She would often sing an old German song, "In Heaven There Is Rest." My mother was always trying to make life easier for everyone else. She was one of the most unselfish people I have ever met. Life had been so hard for her that heaven was truly the only place she would find rest.

At sixty-nine years of age, on March 29,1956, she finally entered that rest. After the funeral we went back to her little house that my brothers had built for her shortly before she died. There we sang songs of heaven for my mother. My mother's sister, Mary, who was still Amish, tearfully said, "I wish my children could have the assurance that I am going to heaven as strongly as you have." And that is one thing I do know. I will spend eternity with my mother!

Years later as I sat to write this book I came upon a poem that mother had given to all of us children. It had been given out as a little pamphlet and she had kept it. This poem describes her own life and this is the legacy she left us.

The Greatest Test

Help me to walk so close to Thee
That those who know me best can see
I live as godly as I pray
And Christ is real from day to day.

I see some once a day, or year,
To them I blameless might appear;
'Tis easy to be kind and sweet
To people whom we seldom meet.

But in my home are those who see
Too many times the worst of me.
My hymns of praise were best unsung
If He does not control my tongue.

When I am vexed and sorely tried
And my impatience cannot hide,
May no one stumble over me
Because Thy love they fail to see.

But give me, Lord, a life that sings
And victory over little things.

Give me Thy calm for every fear,
Thy peace for every falling tear.

Make mine, O Lord, through calm and strife
A gracious and unselfish life;
Help me with those who know me best
For Jesus' sake, to stand the test.
—Barbara C. Ryberg

Each year, on my birthday, Mother's Day, and Father's Day, I talk to God and say, "Father, will you say thank-you to my parents for me and tell them that I understand that it was difficult for them to have a fourteenth child, but I am so grateful that I was born. Thank-you."

Church

Church for us was a solemn occasion with the men sitting on one side of the church and the women on the other. In a lot of churches families did not even sit together. The Sunday sermons often made me aware of my sin which made me very sin-conscious. In my sin-consciousness I could not hear the good news of the Gospel. I felt I had to earn my salvation. Because of that, the revelation that Jesus Christ was my salvation and my righteousness and that I was justified as though I had never sinned, did not soak in until later.

I am often asked who the Mennonites are. I find it difficult to answer this question because there are so many groups of Mennonites. I usually respond by telling about Menno Simmons. Menno left the Catholic Church shortly after Martin Luther did. He believed in baptizing believers only, rather than in infant baptism. Because of this he was labeled Anabaptist.

He also believed that Jesus taught that His kingdom was one of peace; violence in any form, including war, was not a part of it. To support this teaching he used the scripture where Jesus said to Peter, "Put your sword back in its place. For all who draw the sword will die by the sword." He also referred to the scripture in John

23

18:36 where Jesus said, "My kingdom is not of this world. If it were, my servants would fight to prevent my arrest by the Jews. But now my kingdom is from another place." Because of this, Mennonites became known as conscientious objectors, refusing to go to war because of their religious beliefs.

Meeting My Joseph

While in Alden, New York helping my sister, Anna, with her last baby, I met Wallace Kipfer. I was positive that I had found that special man and that he would make me feel better about myself and my self-worth. I was still convinced the real Matilda would be formed and fashioned by people and events outside of herself and the externals of her life would create the feeling of acceptance and love she so longed for.

So, with this unrealistic set of expectations, we were married on April 11, 1948, at the Riverside Mennonite Church in Au Gres, Michigan. Wallace was twenty-five and I was twenty. I was a romantic and was convinced we were going to live happily ever after! Even our names were musical: Wallace and Matilda. The Australian song, "Waltzing Matilda", was popular at the time. Soon I was to find out, however, that Prince Charming wasn't always so charming and I wasn't Cinderella with a glass slipper.

Two years later, on January 18, 1950, our first baby was born. We named our son, Galen Ray Kipfer. Wallace was the proudest daddy in the world and I was so looking forward to motherhood. But the day after our baby's birth I had my first major gallbladder attack. Labor had dislodged the gallstones. The pain was so intense, I thought surely I was going to die. I could not even hold my baby as we drove home from the hospital. My sister, Fannie, took care of my new baby more than I did.

Our doctor sent me to a specialist. Upon entering the door the specialist took one look at me and diagnosed me with gallbladder problems. I had gallstones and a non-functioning gallbladder. It was a relief that they had found the problem, but I felt I had lost valuable time with my baby.

Our next child, Carolyn Joyce, was born July 30, 1951. She was followed by Donald Wayne on November 10,1953, and our daughter, Mary Jane, was born March 29, 1957. Two weeks before our fifth child was born we found out she had died in the womb. Our little Cynthia Ann, a full term baby, was stillborn February 10,1962. Breaking this to our children was one of the most difficult things I have ever had to do. Carolyn, only a few nights before, had dressed her doll in the clothes that Cynthia would wear when we brought her home from the hospital. Eight-year-old Don had been so sure God had heard his prayer and that she would be alive when she was born.

Cynthia's death was one of many unhappy and distressing events that happened. At three years of age Galen had an appendectomy. Carolyn had a blood vessel burst in her stomach, which nearly took her life. Donald was rushed to the hospital with pneumonia. Both of our sons developed Legg Perthes, a very rare disease that causes softening of the hip bone.

It was all to much for me. Sometimes I would tell Wallace there was a curse on us. He would rebuke me and say, "Matilda, don't say that." But the stillborn birth of Cynthia Ann was the last straw. Gradually I began sinking into a deep depression. I was positive that God was very displeased with us.

Depression Manifests Itself

Depression is an insidious thing. It develops so gradually, that it can eventually convince you that you are a failure at everything. I even felt I was a failure as a wife and a mother. How could I have failed at something I had so longed for? Wallace would attempt to encourage and affirm me, but I could not believe even him.

It was extremely difficult for me to receive a compliment. When someone would compliment me I would be embarrassed and try to point out something that I could have done better. When guests would come to dinner and praise me for a good meal, which was indeed delicious, I would respond with, "It didn't turn out like I wanted it to." Yet ironically, I still longed for affirmation and attempted to excel and prove myself, just as I did in grade school. I wanted to wave my "perfect homemaker" report card high in the air, and have someone say, "Matilda, you are the best wife and mother around!"

I hid my depression when others were around, but at home I continually felt like a failure. I never could measure up to my own expectations and my unreasonable standards of motherhood.

When there was trouble in our marriage, I blamed myself because I wasn't the wife I should have been. If there wasn't enough money, I should have managed better or worked harder. I exhausted myself laboring like a man alongside of Wallace in the fields and barns. If the children were having problems, I wasn't spending enough time with them. I was so hard on myself, that, by the end of the day, I was not fun to live with.

Depression intensified and I began to feel my family would be better off if I just wasn't around. I would imagine ways that I could do this so that it would look like an accident and not bring any shame to my family. It was only the fear of God and the love for my family that kept me from making this terrible mistake.

Then in 1958, Wallace's stepbrother Art, who had married my sister Fannie, was killed in a truck accident. Fannie was left to raise five children alone. They were eighteen months to eleven years old. We had thought we knew how to grieve but this took us to a new level. Now we were learning how to truly weep with those who weep and to walk alongside and bear one another's burdens in practical ways. My attention was now focused on them and not on myself.

In the busy weeks and months that followed the accident, my brothers built Fannie a house on our farm. Fannie had to find work and Wallace and I became more than an aunt and uncle. Now, with our combined families, we had nine children. Although they got along very well, they were still normal children. These were difficult times but God's grace was upon us.

We have many happy memories of hay rides, taffy pulls and popcorn balls. I have a cherished picture of Wallace with all nine children on a loaded hay wagon. We dug a pond back by our woods. Wallace brought in three loads of sand for the shallow end and made it a wonderful beach. We roped off the deep end for the non-swimmers and made a diving board for the older children. We had a huge tent that Wallace built a platform under and this became our summer haven and a place of healing. A couple of years later, Fannie remarried and moved to Michigan.

Depression is a symptom of a much deeper problem. It can be triggered by many different things, such as a chemical imbalance, overwork, lack of sleep, or wrong thought patterns. God was about to rearrange my thinking patterns. Jesus made a bold statement when he proclaimed, "If you hold to my teaching, you are really my disciples. Then you will know the truth, and the truth will set you free" (John 8:31,32).

CHAPTER 2

Consumed By His Love

"How do you know that God exists?"
"Is God really more powerful than our circumstances?"
"Why do bad things happen to good people?"

These were questions our son Galen was asking when he arrived home from college. I was alarmed that Galen would challenge God and his questions frightened me. I had a lot of unanswered questions myself. I began to wonder if my Christianity and my life would be enough to lead him to the answers.

As we build a faith of our own these are normal questions that must be answered. I was at a time in my life when I knew the information was true but I didn't have the understanding to make it practical. I knew that I had asked Jesus into my heart and I knew that the Holy Spirit lived in me, but I did not know how to live in the spirit. I was trying to live a faith handed down to me and not of my own. When you read a book or you hear a sermon, the truth that you are hearing must become practical and livable or it just becomes information.

Children need to see a living faith in their parents. Faith must come alive in our spirits and be a natural, everyday part of our lives. The living faith that I had seen in my mother caused me to desire more of God. Her relentless petitioning in prayer had created in me a hunger and a longing to know God as she had.

Around this time I read Hannah Whitehall Smith's book, *The Christians Secret of a Happy Life*. This book began to stir the embers that were getting ready to ignite. I began to realize that I knew Jesus as my Savior but I did not know Him as my Lord. I was so absorbed with myself that I could not comprehend the truth of what He wanted to do in my life.

The young people from our church attended a weekend youth retreat at Beaver Camp, near Lowville, New York. A young man from Flint, Michigan, was the speaker. He and his pilot prayed earnestly for rain so that the young people would not be able to go boating and would have to remain inside. Their prayers were answered. It not only rained outside, but Jesus "reigned" inside as well. When Galen came home, he was a changed man. His face radiated joy. His questions were now answered. He had met with the Holy Spirit and all doubts were gone. A hunger for God's word consumed him.

I asked him, "Who started this revival?"

He looked at me almost shocked, and said, "Why Mom, the Holy Spirit did!"

Effect of Renewal

The next Sunday morning our pastor, Dan Yutzy, asked if any of the youth would care to share their testimony. I could barely believe my eyes when Galen stood and walked to the front of the church. He began to share from the depth of his heart the wonderful change God had worked in him. One by one the young people came forward, some weeping as they shared the reality of their living Lord.

Outward appearance had always been stressed in our church. We were not to conform to the ways of the world. When some of our young men came home from college with long hair and blue jeans, and the girls came home with short hair and shorter skirts, some of the congregation wondered how the experiences described in Acts 2 could have happened to them.

Yet I could not deny that it was real. I was living with one of them! In my heart I knew this was what I had been searching for. They were passionately in love with Jesus and I was passionately yearning to know God like they now knew Him.

My Own Personal Pentecost

One beautiful fall morning the yard was ablaze with color. It was gorgeous! I was in my kitchen canning applesauce and yearning to be ablaze and burning with God's Spirit. From deep within I cried out, "Jesus, You have been my Savior, but this morning I receive You as Lord of my life. I give You this life of mine, with no strings attached." I was momentarily surrounded with light. I immediately thought of Saul and his Damascus road experience. I had never had a divine encounter like this before and it was all so new to me. I knew this had happened in the early church, but I did not understand it could happen in our day.

I sometimes wonder why God gave me such a dramatic experience. And then I think, "Would I have been able to accept the call of God on my life without it?" This experience became a point of reference when later the rejection and ostracism began.

The Lord apprehended me with his Holy Spirit and as I surrendered He began to pour His love into me as wave after wave of love washed over me. I had often quoted the verse, "God is love," but now I knew for certain that He loved me even when I didn't and couldn't love myself. I may not have been planned for but as I was being formed in my mother's womb, He was designing and fashioning a little girl that would bring him much joy. His plans for me were to give me an outstanding journey. I was not a second class citizen. I was not an afterthought. I was not a mistake. If no one else was excited when I was born, He was!

I laughed and cried! I loved myself and I loved Wallace more than when I married him. I was filled with a greater love for my children, the church, the neighbors, the lovely, the unlovely. I loved everyone!

Where had I been! Why did I not know this truth as a child, as a young adult, and as a wife and mother? What a difference it would have made in my life!

Love was my first evidence of being baptized with the Holy Spirit. Second was a hunger for the Word of God and third, I began to understand how to make it practical in my life. I read my Bible with a new set of eyeglasses. It almost seemed as though I was reading it for the first time. Each day the scripture was new and fresh and filled me with wonder and life.

The work of the Holy Spirit is to reveal Jesus to us so we can know the Father. The Holy Spirit began to just open up the Word of God and introduce me to women that Jesus had set free. I began to understand that God valued women as well as men.

One of the first stories He led me to was Luke 13:10-17. As I read this story I wondered why I had not seen this before.

I don't recall ever hearing a sermon about this woman. She met Jesus in the synagogue on a Sabbath day. Life had been hard for her and for eighteen years she had been unable to stand straight. Jesus called her before the rulers of the synagogue, and laid His hands on her, and set her free from her infirmities. Immediately she realized she was born to praise and worship God. She was so overwhelmed; she had touched life! Jesus came to set us free and He had set her free. Indignant rulers of the synagogue tried to silence her but Jesus defended her and declared her a daughter of Abraham, worth far more than their valued animals. Jesus challenged them with that truth.

Verse 17 states that His adversaries were put to shame. "And all the multitude rejoiced for all the glorious things that were done by Him" (NKJV) One woman had touched truth and her future was changed forever.

In verse 20 Jesus asks, "To what shall I liken the kingdom of God? It is like leaven, which a woman took and hid in three measures of meal till it was all leavened" (NKJV). Here He is saying that truth in a woman is just as powerful as it is in a man and it will affect the home, the church, and the world.

In Luke 8:43-48 there was a woman with an issue of blood who broke the religious law of her day. This woman should not have been with a crowd of people, let alone touch a rabbi or any religious leader in her condition. But in her desperation, she knew that Jesus was her only hope. She had spent all of her money trying to get well and so she pressed in for just a touch of the hem of Jesus' garment. Fear gripped her when Jesus said "Who touched me?" Peter and those with him said, "Master, the people are crowding and pressing against you." Jesus had felt her faith draw power from him and He said to the fearful woman, "Daughter, be of good cheer; your faith has made you well" (NKJV)

In John 8:1-11, we read the story of the woman taken in adultery. Truly she was guilty for she had been caught in the very act. Jesus didn't single her out to die, but caused every man to examine his own heart. One by one, under the conviction of the Word, each man left and He, the King of glory, the only one who could have condemned her, let her go.

One day as I was reading the story of the resurrection in John chapter 20, I met Mary Magdalen. The other gospels say there were other women with her, but her name is mentioned first in all the accounts. She had been a very troubled woman. Jesus had cast two demons out of her. According to Luke's account. Mary, along with other women whom Jesus had healed and set free, followed Jesus and his disciples from village to village, ministering to their needs.

Matthew, in describing the crucifixion in chapter 27, verse 55, stated that many women were watching from a distance. They had followed Jesus from Galilee to minister to His needs. Again, Mary's name is mentioned first. The disciples had scattered, but not the women. They had touched the extravagant love of God and had followed Jesus to His death and, according to verse 61, even to His tomb.

Mary Magdalen and the other Mary, the mother of James, watched as His body was laid to rest. Early on the first day of the week, while it was still dark (and the disciples were behind closed doors), the women went to the tomb. I have a very active imagination and I love to imagine the scene. Seeing the stone rolled away, and his body gone, they quickly ran to the disciples and said, "They have taken the Lord out of the tomb" (John 20:2). The disciples didn't really believe them but at least Peter and John went to check it out.

When they arrived they saw the truth, that the women were right. Jesus' body was not there. The disciples went back home, but Mary Magdalen remained there. She was standing at the tomb weeping and when she bent over to look one more time she saw two angels. They asked her why she was crying and her answer is absolutely breathtaking.

"They have taken my Lord away and I don't know where they have put Him." Turning around she saw Jesus, and He said to her, "Woman, why are you crying? Who is it you are looking for?" And she, thinking he was the gardener, said, "Sir, if you have carried him away, tell me where you have put him, and I will get him."

Had the disciples gone home too soon, or did He deliberately plan to reveal Himself to a woman first? I do know extravagant love always brings God on the scene. Even though she saw Him die and saw Him buried, she called Him "my Lord." To love God like that is my heart's cry. In the face of what looks impossible I want to still say, "My Lord" as well.

Jesus said to her, "Mary," and the scales fell from her eyes and she reached for Him. He said, "Do not hold on to me, for I have not yet returned to the Father. Go instead to my brothers and tell them, 'I am returning to my Father and your Father, to My God and your God'" (John 20:17).

Have you ever wondered if He pointed at her when He said, "My Father and your Father, My God and your God." The greatest news the world has ever heard, "He is risen!", was to be delivered by a woman. If it is wrong for women to share the good news with men then God has contradicted Himself.

Oh yes, I was beginning to see what God thought about women. He loved them. He had compassion on them and mercy for them. He straightened them up, healed their infirmities, and forgave their sins. And I, Matilda, was now one of those straightened, healed and forgiven women.

More Blessings of the Renewal

In November of 1971, the same young man who had ministered to our young people came to our church for our annual Thanksgiving weekend renewal. Pastor Dan and Martha Yutzy and many others, including my daughters Mary Jane and Carolyn, came into the baptism of the Holy Spirit during this weekend. Pastor Yutzy was an outstanding man of God, but once he received this baptism it brought an even greater spiritual dimension into his life.

Church prayer meetings, and Bible Study all took on a new meaning for me. I declared the sky was bluer, and the grass greener. Even the birds rejoiced with me. Oh, how I wanted to sing again, to raise my voice in worship to God. But for some time that had not been possible. When I was younger, we had sung so much as a family that I had developed two growths on my vocal cords. The doctor told me that I should not sing or raise my voice for a while.

On this particular Sunday night, I felt a release in my throat. I was so in love with God that I had to express this extravagant love to Him. As I sang, I knew that God had healed me. Pastor Dan encouraged me to go to the doctor and have him check my throat.

"My goodness, Matilda, what did you do, The growths are all gone," said the throat specialist. God knew I needed my voice for His assignment.

God was preparing me for ministry long before I was aware of His plan. Not long after this Wallace said, "I haven't heard you complaining about your arthritis lately." It dawned on me that I no longer had aching joints. I was so absorbed in my new love relationship that my attention was no longer on myself.

Not Everyone Understood

Not everyone was as excited as I was with my Damascus Road experience. I began to share my experience with my dear sister-in-law. I was sure she would understand; we were as close as sisters. But as I began sharing, a wall of separation developed between us. Our relationship became one of courtesy, no longer intimate.

I knew born again Christians had the Holy Spirit but I was sure that not everyone had experienced the Lordship of Jesus Christ. In my exuberance about this new revelation I made many mistakes. I asked a dear brother, Pastor John Garlington, "Why am I turning people off?"

He said, "Matilda, don't be a gusher. A gusher is easy to find. Go into your church and leak. A leak is much harder to find."

This sounded like a modern day version of Matthew 10, a scripture which had been coming to me for quite sometime, especially the second part of verse 16: "Therefore be as shrewd as snakes and as innocent as doves."

A member of my family, out of love and concern, came to the house and said, "Matilda, this is heresy. You need to renounce this." I replied that I could never do that, even if they excommunicated me. I was willing to pay the price.

What I was experiencing was a life changing event. It was not just out of my emotions as some were saying. This was real! As truth went from facts in my head to truth in my heart, it did pass through and affect my emotions. But I also knew without a doubt that this went much deeper than emotions.

For years I had lived out of the emotions of fear, timidity, self-consciousness, and defensiveness. I really did not know how to reach beyond my emotions and live out of truth. Now that I realized His love was abiding in me, it certainly did affect my emotions; there was no doubt about it!

Truth began to burn inside of me like fire. Yet I needed to be wise in how I shared this truth with others. Truth anchors our souls (will and emotions) and sets us free. As I kept bitterness and unforgiveness out of my own heart God opened up His doors for me to share His truth with others.

There have been a few times as I have been writing this book that I have felt so overwhelmed and have asked myself, "What do you think you are doing!" And then I remember. I am writing His story with my unique personality in obedience to His will. I can do all things in and because of His mighty strength in me.

The Work of the Holy Spirit

One morning as I was reading Genesis 3, I began to realize that before man sinned he was God conscious, fearless and teachable. Now by God-conscious I mean that man was in perfect relationship with God and he was absorbed with God and not himself. He was perfect in thought and action and relationship with God and his wife. After they sinned they became self-conscious, fearful and defensive. The work of the Holy Spirit in the believer is a progressive revelation of Jesus Christ who desired to restore the three things Adam lost.

Before Adam and Eve sinned they were undefiled, sinless people. God would come in the cool of the day and have intimate fellowship with them. After they disobeyed God, the Spirit of God left them.

Jesus, the last Adam, came as a man totally God-conscious, fearless and teachable. He always did and said what He saw His Father doing and saying. He never defended Himself, because there was no need to do so. He was secure in who He was, the Son of God. The more we know that we too are sons and daughters of the Most High God, the more secure we become and the less we need to defend ourselves. I am so thankful that this is an ongoing process and that God Himself oversees the process with His abundant love and mercy.

CHAPTER 3

Passing Through the Valley of Baca

One day Galen walked into the house and said, "Mom, I feel God wants a coffee house ministry in Alden. I even know what building."

Galen, along with some other young people, had shared this vision earlier with our Pastor Dan Yutzy, but no one had known how to take the steps to begin. Not knowing what he should do he decided to go to Harrisonburg, Virginia, where his girlfriend Debbie Hess was attending Eastern Mennonite College.

It was November and our church was in revival. The young man who had ministered to the young people in June was now holding meetings during the Thanksgiving weekend. My dear friend, Becky Bontrager, was deeply touched by the Holy Spirit during these meetings.

One evening sleep eluded her and she slipped out of bed, curled up in a chair, and began to read an article in the Reader's Digest about coffee houses. As she read, a deep sense arose within her that God wanted a Christian coffee house in Alden.

"Why are you telling me this? I am nobody, God! The coffee house has been talked about before and nothing ever happened. Dear God, what do you want from me?" asked Becky.

She heard, "I'll do it. I know you can't."

After a few minutes of struggling Becky surrendered. "God, if I can do something about a coffee house, or if You want to do something through me, you'll have to speak very clearly."

A peace settled over her as she spoke. God was so real and so near that the room was filled with His presence. She began to ask more questions, specific questions, and to take notes, just like a secretary would do.

"Lord, where would we get the money?" she asked.

He answered immediately, "The five hundred dollars your mother gave you before she died."

"Lord, what building would we use?"

Again the answer was swift and to the point, "The building where the Baptist Church used to meet."

By now, Becky could barely contain her excitement. "Who would help and who shall I share this with, Lord? I need someone to pray with me and I need confirmation."

"Share it with Matilda, and she will pray with you."

Becky had never experienced this kind of sweet fellowship before. She suddenly asked, "Jesus, would you like to have a cup of tea with me?"

At the time, it did not seem like a strange request to make. He was there, she was thirsty, and His presence was so real as He shared His heart and plans.

She found two cups and prepared the tea. Then she added sugar to hers.

"I need sugar in mine, but Jesus you are sweet enough. You don't need sugar," she said.

Suddenly an awe, a holy fear, came over her as she looked at the other cup and said, "No, God! Don't drink the tea in your cup, I don't think I could stand it."

At that moment she realized just how finite she was compared to His infinite power and love. She later wondered what greater joy she might have known, had she not feared that the power and the beauty of God would consume her. She determined that if the opportunity arose again, her immediate response would be, "I am the Lord's servant. May it be to me as you have said."

Expanding the Vision

The next morning Becky had more questions and was gently reminded to go slowly. "In quietness and confidence shall be your strength" Isaiah 30:15 (NKJV).

She knew that she was going to need her husband's support and his help. How should she approach him? He, more than anyone else, knew her weaknesses and past failures.

"God," she prayed, "you will have to prepare his heart and give me wisdom to know how to present your plan to him wisely."

Her first thought was to rush to my house and tell me everything, but God held her back. "Go slow and easy, Becky," He reminded her. "I'll tell you when. I will direct every detail."

During the Wednesday evening prayer meeting, December 1, 1971, God began to confirm His word. Becky approached me and said, "Matilda, you can't believe what God is asking me to do!"

"Start a coffee house!" I quickly replied.

We laughed, cried and rejoiced! She shared with me her story and I shared with her Galen's burden and vision. Becky and Galen had envisioned the coffee house in the same building. What a confirmation!

Later, when Becky felt it was time to tell her husband John, he was responsive and positive. She asked him for help and he responded with, "I'll take you to downtown Buffalo to visit another Christian coffee house."

On December 11, Becky shared her vision with Pastor Dan and his wife Martha. Before Becky could get the words out of her mouth, Martha already knew what she was going to say. Once again God's confirmation came through the body of believers. He was at work.

Taking It to the Church

Pastor Dan suggested to Becky that she share with the congregation what God had shown her and invite anyone who was interested in the coffee house to come to her home that evening after church.

Pastor Dan led the meeting and we discussed whether God was asking our church to be involved in a coffee house ministry in the village. After a time, Dan called the people to prayer. The air was charged with the presence of God and I will never forget that night as long as I live. After experiencing this I could understand how great men of prayer could forget about time and pray all night.

A consensus was reached and the group was in agreement! God wanted us to have a coffee house in the village. Now where would it be? Suggestions started flying. One man offered his basement. My nephew Alfred, a real estate broker, suggested another building. Again, Pastor Dan called us to prayer. Dan knew the building, for he had heard Becky's story, but he was waiting for God to reveal it to the church.

Becky began to pray aloud, "Lord, I believe you have shown me the building and if that's the one, please confirm it to someone right now."

We waited for a moment and then my nephew spoke again, "Lord, it comes to me now that this building…" Then he named the building.

The Spirit of God was moving hearts. People later could not even believe that they had given their consent. I had never been to a prayer meeting where the air was so charged with the presence of God.

Coffee Anyone?

One morning soon after our meeting Becky went to the post office and saw the owner of the building come walking toward her on the stairs. She asked him about the building and he stated that he would only sell the building to our church.

On Sunday night, January 30, 1972, the church met to vote on purchasing the building. Galen had come home from Virginia for the purpose of sharing his vision for the coffee house. After he had shared, another young man who taught school in the public school system stood and shared his opinion. His reasons for not having a coffee house were excellent. I was impressed with his explanation and could understand his concerns.

Earlier that morning our assistant pastor had gone to Wallace and expressed his opinion that the timing was not right for the coffee house. Was he right?

As the discussion continued at the meeting, Pastor Dan spoke. "We have discussed this enough. It is time to pray. Let's kneel." The atmosphere was electrifying as we knelt at our benches.

Suddenly, the teacher who had given all the great reasons why we should not have a coffee house prayed aloud, "Lord, I make a motion the church buy that building for a coffee house."

The assistant pastor, who had felt the timing was wrong, replied, "I second the motion."

I was kneeling at the time and could barely contain myself. I had never heard anyone do business with God in this manner before, nor have I ever heard of it since!

Changed Lives, Our Own Included

The church bought the building. Galen married his sweetheart, Debbie, and they moved to Alden to an apartment above the new ministry appropriately named, *Coffee House*. Thus the outreach began that would forever change our lives.

Galen was chosen to head the coffee house ministry, but not without opposition. There were many opinions on how to operate the house and who should run it. But in spite of it all, God blessed this outreach and young people came in by the droves.

The village was considered small, but the needs were staggering. Young men and women were saved, but Satan worked overtime trying to prevent God's purposes from being accomplished. And all of us, in the middle of the fray, needed to learn so much.

One Saturday night at the Coffee House a young man named Sunshine spoke. Galen had heard about this young man and had asked him to share his testimony. The Spirit of the Lord came upon those present. A basket was placed in the front and many came forward and threw in their cigarettes, needles and other drug paraphernalia.

Wallace and I were on the church's Sunday evening program committee at the time and we had an opening for the Sunday night service. We invited Sunshine to share at the church service. With him came eight of the young people who had received Christ the night before. They came with their blue jeans and ponytails, smelling of cigarettes and looking unkempt. They looked more rebellious than sanctified to many who saw them enter that night.

A man stood up and said, "If Jesus were here tonight, He would do just what He did in the temple. He would take a whip and cleanse this place."

Whenever I return to that evening in my memory, my heart breaks, for upon hearing this and feeling the rejection, these young people walked out of the church and said, "There is nothing to this at all." They returned to their previous lifestyles.

I was hoping it was all a bad dream, but it wasn't. As far as we know at the time of this writing, none of those who walked out that night are walking with the Lord.

After that evening it is so hard to say what all happened. Some began to think that Galen should not head up the coffee house ministry. Confusion set in and discouragement overwhelmed us. Galen and Debbie were starting their marriage in this setting and precious little Gretchen, our first grandchild, was born into it. So many adjustments had to be made. So many personality clashes needed to be worked through. Satan used every weapon he could muster to crush this work.

Enough Is Enough

At one point, when Galen and Debbie went to Pennsylvania for a much needed rest, I went to the Coffee House to water the plants. I locked the door behind me and had it out with God. I laid on the floor crying out for understanding.

"Father, I must know. Did we hear you right? Is Galen really your choice or did we imagine it?"

I spent a long time on my face seeking the Lord for an answer. After a time I felt led to turn to Psalm 131. David had such a way of expressing his feelings. It was exactly how I felt.

"My heart is not proud, O Lord, my eyes are not haughty; I do not concern myself with great matters or things too wonderful for me. But I have stilled and quieted my soul; like a weaned child with its mother, like a weaned child is my soul within me. O Israel put your hope in the Lord both now and forevermore" (Psalm 131).

The following Sunday afternoon, after Galen and Debbie returned from their trip, Galen had a strong desire to go to a Sunday evening service at the Full Gospel Tabernacle in Orchard Park. A visiting speaker called Galen out of the crowd. "Young man," he said, "are you aware that God has called you to minister to young people..."

The next morning a brother from the church called and asked, "Do you know what happened to Galen last night?"

It was some time before Galen shared the impact of that night with me. I had asked God for confirmation for I needed to know that it was not a figment of my imagination that Galen was God's choice. He had picked His man and ordained the one He had chosen for that particular hour in that particular place. We were on the right track!

I am sorry to admit that I told God this assignment for my family was more than we could bear, but I did. There is so much I cannot even explain now. I only know God chose us to walk through a valley of darkness while He taught us life changing principles that would change lives all over the world. We were often misunderstood and our words misinterpreted, but our warfare was never against people, but against the principalities and powers of darkness. We made many mistakes but God has kept His hands on us. In spite of it all God blessed this outreach. I know of several who found salvation at the Coffee House that are in the ministry today. Galen still receives phone calls from young people thanking him because of the work at the Coffee House.

Wednesday Bible Study

A neighborhood Bible study began in our home but soon became too large for our house. I asked our new pastor if we could meet in the Coffee House.

Every week new women were coming and being saved. They would go home so changed that their husbands would begin to attend. I was always taught that women were not to teach men. I called our pastor and shared my dilemma. It didn't seem right that I should stop men from getting saved and he really didn't know what to do either so... We kept on going and they kept on coming.

There were times after the Bible study that I would sit there in a daze. I wondered where this was going to lead me. We saw miracle after miracle. We would pray for people and they would go back to the doctor and their cancers would be gone. We would write prayer needs on a blackboard, lay our hands on them and agree in prayer, and "signs and wonders" would follow.

Many of the people who were coming to the Bible study had never been in a church and some who had were no longer welcome in their church after being filled with the Holy Spirit. They needed to become part of a church body and our church was not able to receive these people. We had outgrown the Coffee House and businesses were complaining because there were no parking spaces for their customers. These people needed a church.

One of the men who had been saved and filled with the Holy Spirit owned one of the largest concrete businesses in western New York. He also was no longer welcome in his church. With his help a building was purchased. Galen was eventually ordained as pastor of the new church, which he pastored for over ten years. The church is still there today and is called Alden Community Fellowship.

One of the many things that God taught us is that we are pilgrims and not campers. We do not camp beside the hurtful things of life or the things we do not understand. We must keep walking!

"How blessed is the man whose strength is in Thee;
In whose heart are the highways to Zion!
Passing through the valley of Baca, they make it a
    spring,
The early rain also covers it with blessings.
They go from strength to strength,
every one of them appears before God in Zion.
O Lord God of hosts, hear my prayer;
Give ear, O God of Jacob! Selah.
Behold our shield, O God,
And look upon the face of Thine anointed.
For a day in Thy courts is better than a thousand
    outside.
I would rather stand at the threshold of the house of

my God,
Than dwell in the tents of wickedness.
For the Lord God is a sun and shield;
The Lord gives grace and glory;
No good thing does He withhold from those who
walk uprightly.
O Lord of hosts, How blessed is the man who trusts
in Thee!"
(Psalm 84:5-12 NAS)

I love how Eugene Peterson translates verses 4 and 5, "And how blessed all those in whom you live, whose lives become roads you travel; They wind through lonesome valleys, come upon brooks, discover cool springs and pools brimming with rain! God-traveled, these roads curve up the mountain, and at last turn—Zion! God in full view!"

So Pilgrim, keep walking! I have heard it said, "When life hands you a lemon, make lemonade. When you feel like you are in the pits, dig a well." You can refresh the thirsty coming along after you. We are living for those who are traveling behind us. When we plant a tree, the full benefit of that shade, coolness, and protection, will not be known by us, but will be known by the next generation and those following. So choose and plant well. They will find the journey tiring and good directions will be needed. By following your lead they shall soon be home.

CHAPTER 4

Law of the Spirit of Life

"Therefore, there is now no condemnation for those who are in Christ Jesus, because through Christ Jesus the law of the Spirit of life set me free from the law of sin and death" (Romans 8:1-2).

Every day we are writing a testimony with how we handle discord and disappointments and fight those day to day battles in the workplace, our marriages, our church life, and our world. Operating in the law of the spirit of life will give us victory in these situations. We do not fight empty handed. God has given His warriors armor and every piece of that armor is Jesus Himself. Armor that has already been tried and is victorious. Jesus-the helmet of our salvation. Jesus-our righteousness. Jesus-our shield of faith. Jesus-the belt of truth. Jesus-the sword of the Spirit and Jesus-the Prince of Peace.

In Deuteronomy 30, God sets before Israel a choice of life or death, of prosperity or destruction. They were to obey the Lord and follow His commands. In verses 11-14, He tells them, "Now what I am commanding you today is not too difficult for you or beyond your reach. It is not up in heaven, so that you have to ask, 'Who will ascend into heaven to get it and proclaim it to us so we may obey it?' Nor is it beyond the sea, so that you have to ask, 'Who will cross the sea to get it and proclaim it to us so we may obey it?' No, the word is very near you; it is in your mouth and in your heart so you may obey it." (Paul quoted this scripture in Romans 10:6-8.)

Deuteronomy 30:15,16 says, "See, I set before you today life and prosperity, death and destruction. For I command you today to love the Lord your God, to walk in His ways, and to keep his commands, decrees and laws; then you will live and increase, and the Lord your God will bless you in the land you are entering to possess."

In verse 19 he emphasizes this even more. "This day I call heaven and earth as witnesses against you that I have set before you life and death, blessings and curses. Now choose life, so that you and your children may live…"

The more opposition I faced the more I saw my need to choose this law of life. I knew the Word said that no weapon formed against me would prosper and every tongue raised against me I would prove to be in the wrong through the law of life. There was no denying the hurt, the loneliness, the fear and the temptation to defend myself. But as I tried to explain, it only created more rejection. So I asked the Holy Spirit to teach me how to walk in the spirit instead of the flesh.

Now God could show me the areas in my life that needed changing. The process of renewing my mind was crucial if I ever wanted victory. I knew that I was a pauper in the flesh and victory lay in the Lordship of Jesus Christ and His life within me was the answer. I had His love, joy, peace, longsuffering, gentleness, goodness, faith, meekness, and self-control in me. Now He was enrolling me into the school of the Holy Spirit.

In my early morning devotions I was reading Matthew 5, which records the Beatitudes. In verses 10-12, I read, "Blessed are those who are persecuted because of righteousness, for theirs is the kingdom of heaven.

Blessed are you when people insult you, persecute you and falsely say all kinds of evil against you because of me.

Rejoice and be glad, because great is your reward in heaven, for in the same way they persecuted the prophets who were before you."

In Luke 6:22-23 we read, "Blessed are you when men hate you, when they exclude you and insult you and reject your name as evil, because of the Son of Man. Rejoice in that day and leap for joy, because great is your reward in heaven. For that is how their fathers treated the prophets."

I said, "Father, I don't feel like being exceedingly glad and I sure don't feel like leaping for joy. Furthermore, I know you don't tell me to jump just to see how high I can jump. There is a truth here I need to understand. If you will show me why and how, I will obey."

Paul prayed in Philippians 3:10, "I want to know Christ and the power of his resurrection and the fellowship of sharing in his sufferings..." The last part was hard for me to say. I did not like that word *suffering!*

We do not fight this battle with carnal flesh but with the same power that raised Christ from the dead. We are warriors and every piece of the armor is Jesus. The Holy Spirit began to give me understanding. God's love is shed abroad in my heart and I want to confess that with my mouth no matter what my circumstances.

Jesus hung on the cross and all hell thought they had won. But when he cried, "IT IS FINISHED," it set off an earthquake so horrendous that even the centurion said, "Surely this was the Son of God." When he cried, "FATHER, FORGIVE THEM FOR THEY DO NOT KNOW WHAT THEY ARE DOING," He set into motion a law so powerful that three thousand of those scoundrels were saved on the day of Pentecost.

I believe whenever I forgive, the same law is released and it has the same power to save. It worked that way for Stephen as we can see in Acts 6,7, and 9. The stones were flying and he released the same law when he cried, "Lord, do not hold this sin against them." Those words turned a Saul into a powerful Paul!

Paul then released this law while in a prison, along with Silas. As their backs were bleeding, and their feet were in stocks, they began to sing and praise God. The law was so perfect it set off another earthquake and this time the jailer and all his household were saved.

In James 1:25 we read, "But the man who looks intently into the perfect law that gives freedom, and continues to do this, not forgetting what he has heard, but doing it—he will be blessed in what he does."

James 2:12-13 says, "Speak and act as those who are going to be judged by the law that gives freedom, because judgment without mercy will be shown to anyone who has not been merciful. Mercy triumphs over judgment!"

I wept that morning as I saw truth unfold before my very eyes. I had heard many sermons on forgiveness but now I had understanding. You do not forgive out of emotions but from the heart. Our hearts are where God dwells. Isaiah 12:3 refers to us as wells of salvation. Isaiah says that in that day we would draw water out of those wells and we would praise the Lord.

I knew I had the life of God in me. I now needed to exercise my will and go past my emotions. By faith I reached into the well, and with my mouth I declared the answer instead of the problem. I was about to have a circumstance to which I could apply this principle.

My in-laws from Michigan decided to visit us. At the time, I was in New Jersey speaking at a ladies' meeting. When I came home, my son and husband told me all that Grandma had said. It wasn't nice. We were an absolute embarrassment to her. She felt my place was at home. My husband, who is a gentle man, described it as really bad, and my son said, "I will never set my foot in Grandma's house again."

With my coat still on, and the anger rising in my flesh, I said out loud, "Father, I thank you that your love is in my heart. I go past my feelings and down into my spirit and I pray when the books are opened and what Mom did to me is seen, strike it off her record. When you rose from the dead and appeared to the disciples in John 20:23, you breathed on them and said, 'Receive the Holy Spirit.' If you forgive his sins they are forgiven; if you do not forgive them, they are not forgiven.' I forgive Mom."

I still felt anger but before an hour was up, I wrote her a letter out of my spirit, not out of the anger I was feeling. I gave it to my husband to read. He said it was good and that I could send it.

On the way to the mailbox I kept saying, "When Mom reads this it will bring life, unity and reconciliation." I was still struggling with anger. But after I put the letter into the mailbox and turned to come into the house, I heard heaven cheer! I can't be sure whether it was in the spirit or if it was audible but I heard it. I heard, "SHE DID IT! SHE DID IT! Matilda is learning to walk in the spirit and not in the flesh."

I felt my mother and father were in the crowd cheering that morning. I ran into the house and grabbed the first Bible I could find and I read Hebrews 12:1: "Therefore, since we are surrounded by such a great cloud of witnesses... let us run with perseverance the race marked out for us..."

For some time I didn't share that story for fear someone would trample it. But I began to pray for Mom everyday. Whenever the thought of what she had said would come to me I would again release life to her and say, "It really doesn't matter what she said. All that matters is that I get to release life to her."

Years later she stood in my kitchen and with tears in her eyes said, "If only I could recall those words." And I replied, "Mom, those were under the blood long ago."

Giving Life

My brother and his family lived with us while their house was being built. My niece, who was very young, took money out of our son's piggy bank. Her folks took care of the matter but whenever she was around me she would feel shame.

She had moved to Arizona and whenever they would come back to New York to visit she would be in and out before I even knew she had been there. At one of the family gatherings her rejection of me was very obvious. It was clear that I must have done something that hurt her deeply. It was so bad that others noticed and commented on it.

I spoke to God about my pain. He reminded me of the times we would go blueberry picking in Michigan. I was very competitive and when I would find a patch with big berries, I wouldn't tell anyone. I wanted to fill my pail first.

God reminded me in Matthew 5:7 that the merciful obtain mercy. I knew I needed all the mercy I could get. Mercy, given out of my Spirit, was like a fruit. When I gave mercy to others it was like filling my pail with fruit. The bigger the hurt the bigger the mercy berries. Now I could fill up my bucket very quickly and I would have enough for my family and lots to give away. The more I gave, the more I would obtain. I put my niece and her family on my prayer list and the list became my berry patch. As the hurts came, the list grew larger.

I had earned enough air miles for two free tickets. Wallace and I decided to fly to Arizona. I had been praying for my niece a few years now and I felt this was going to be the time for our reconciliation. At a family gathering I asked my niece for a few moments of her time. I said to her, "Somewhere in life I have hurt you and I want to ask you to forgive me because I can't even remember when or how."

She fell into my arms and said, "Aunt Matilda, I have never loved myself and every time I get around you I think of the money I took out of Galen's bank." That day a little girl was set free. Today that niece and I do retreats together. We laugh and we share with other women the power of the cross and the Lord's resurrection power inside of us!

We were living in western New York State when the Lord was teaching me these truths. One day I was on my way to Woodstock, Ontario Canada, to do some leadership training. I was serving as a field representative for a worldwide Christian women's organization called Aglow. I was all alone in the car and feeling very ordinary but as I traveled the Queen Elizabeth Highway I gathered my mercy berries. I prayed for individuals and for churches. In those earlier days I was a very controversial name in the Mennonite church and the treatment I received as a woman often made my mercy buckets fill up quickly!

I was in prayer with my eyes wide open. I was not feeling super spiritual and I had no Holy Ghost goose bumps. Suddenly I sensed the car filling up with the glory of God. I knew that prayer was the most powerful way to release the ministry of Jesus. I also knew that every person was given the privilege of prayer. I was so overwhelmed with God's presence and with the power of prayer that I must have followed a car off one of the exits. I realized I was in a town I didn't know Canada even had. I pulled into a gas station. A young man had just finished servicing a car and was walking towards me. Suddenly he stopped, and with the most astounded look on his face, he pointed a finger at me and said, "Lady, will you promise me you will always stay as beautiful as you are right now?"

Now I know I wouldn't win a beauty contest, but I truly believe my face shown with the glory of God. I had touched the heart of God through prayer.

The law of the Spirit of life, my friend, is for living. It is for every aspect of the journey. No wonder hell hopes we never learn how to choose life because the life Jesus released in us still sets off earthquakes and brings people out of the graves of bondage.

Everyday Miracles

Our children went to Eastern Mennonite High School in Harrisonburg, Virginia, for the last two years of their high school education. While there, our third child Don, made some wrong choices. Many times I feared we were losing him. If we tried to correct him he would threaten to move in with his friends. I was learning a lot about spiritual warfare on the home front. The Lord continued to teach me how to release life instead of death and how to live out of the promise instead of the problem.

I released the spirit of life into Don as I cooked, cleaned and washed for him. I prayed over his clothing as I folded and ironed it. I figured if Peter could pray over clothes and people were healed when they touched them, then I too could release the same power. I would make his bed and lay my hands over it praying that as he slept God would give him dreams. He did have dreams. One was that Jesus came back and he was left behind.

I would speak over his music and declare that its power over his mind was broken. I would get so happy praying that I would say, "Ha, Ha!" God had instructed me to agree with Him about my family. I knew there was no one I would rather agree with than God. I looked up the word *children* in my concordance and changed my prayer life. I began to pray God's promises with thanksgiving instead of reminding Him of my problems. What a difference it made in my faith!

Examples of Praying the Word over Our Children

I thank You, Father God, that You promised to pour out Your

Spirit on my sons and my daughters and they would prophesy, and our young men would see visions. (See Joel 2:28.)

I thank You that my children are my inheritance and my reward. (See Psalm 127:3.)

I thank You that my children are taught of the Lord and great is their peace. (See Isaiah 54:13.)

No weapon formed against my family will prosper and every tongue that is raised against us, we will prove to be in the wrong. (See Isaiah 54:17.)

You said, "'As for me, this is my covenant with them,' says the Lord, " 'My Spirit, who is on you, and my words that I have put in your mouth will not depart from your mouth, or from the mouths of your children, or from the mouths of their descendants from this time on and forever,' says the Lord" (Isaiah 59:21.)

Your promise is for me and for my children. (See Acts 2:39.)

By faith I do receive Your promise. (See Galatians 3:14.)

You are not slow in keeping Your promise. (See 2 Peter 3:9.)

My heart will not be troubled, I will trust in God, I thank You it is impossible for You to lie!

The Power of God in Us

God instructed me to go home and be fun to live with. One evening Don came home from work and put his arm around my shoulders. He said, "Mom, you are fun to live with." Those were the most life-giving words I had ever heard. Soon after that, Don gave his heart to the Lord while up in his bed. Later I found his records beside the garbage can, ready to go to the city dump.

I shared the story of Don and the power of God's life in us at an Aglow meeting in Oneonta, New York. There was a woman there whose son was dealing drugs. She had preached her sermons, begged, and cried her tears but nothing penetrated. She went home from that meeting armed for battle. She had the Spirit of life living in her.

She took her autoharp and went up to her son Chuck's bedroom where she began to sing and praise God. She too was a daughter of promise, with the same Spirit I had. The grandmother had also heard me and joined in agreement with her daughter.

Chuck decided to go to a Rolling Stones concert in Buffalo, New York but that didn't throw his mother or grandmother. They were home, praising God that life was much more powerful than death. While Chuck was sitting in the concert with his friends, the scales fell off his eyes and he saw the horrible wickedness he was in. He gave his heart to the Lord right there at the concert.

I told Chuck's story at a large Aglow International Conference in California. There was a delegation of women from England who had just heard the secretary for the manager of the Rolling Stones give her testimony. She had become a Christian and, not knowing what else to do, continued her job. While the Stones were doing their concert in Buffalo, New York, she went behind the curtains and prayed that someone would get saved. Can you imagine how she felt when the ladies shared Chuck's story!

Last summer I received a call from Chuck. He was going to preach his first sermon and invited us to be there. We were not able to go but what a thrill to hear the sequels to God's stories.

I said earlier that this law is for every day use. Whenever and wherever it is released it will break up fallow ground. Jesus said, "The words I have spoken to you are spirit and they are life" (John 6:63). In Jeremiah 23:29 God said, "Is not my word like fire,' declares the Lord, 'and like a hammer that breaks a rock in pieces?'"

An Old Tractor and a New Marriage

The insecurities Wallace and I brought to our marriage became strongholds in our relationship. We had both viewed marriage as a way to fill the voids within us. One problem that would cause dissension was that Wallace would make independent decisions. He would buy things such as cars or tractors and drive them into the yard and surprise me. I wanted to be part of his life and share in the decisions about money matters. I had grown up in a very frugal household and never wanted to be poor. I hated debt with a passion and worked hard to avoid it.

Wallace had been in partnership with his father and two brothers until he was twenty-nine years old. Throughout that time he had never made any of the decisions. When we were married, he had a need to take control. Not having had it modeled for him, it was very difficult for him to recognize the need for another person's input. Counsel was often the last thing he sought. Learning by trial and error is a process and this process is usually started before marriage when a mistake isn't quite as serious.

I hated my reactions and I prayed, "Father, burn that out of me. I want to respond instead of react."

We sold our dairy and we rented out the land, so when Wallace said he would like to buy a tractor, I for the life of me, saw no need for one. But Wallace went out and bought a nine thousand dollar tractor from a private owner.

I was not upset!! God had changed me, but I did not realize it yet.

Two weeks later he came home looking terrible. I asked, "Wallace, what happened?"

"Nothing," he replied.

The next morning he even looked worse. "Wallace, if we have learned anything in our marriage, we have learned we need to be open and honest. What happened?"

"Are you sure you can handle it?" he asked.

What... me overreact! I calmly assured him that I could handle it. He proceeded to tell me that the tractor had broken in half. Out of my innermost being came these words, "Big Deal! That is just a piece of steel."

Suddenly I realized God had changed me. Right then and there I had a praise session. "Bless God I am not the same woman I used to be. It is worth nine thousand dollars just to know that you are changing me and answering my prayers."

It was going to cost twenty-six hundred dollars to get it fixed. We didn't have the money but I was still not upset.

We put the tractor in the repair shop and flew together to Anchorage, Alaska, where I was to speak at an Aglow area retreat. The presence of God was so evident at this retreat that both the leadership and I are sure we heard angelic voices singing during the worship. I actually stopped and listened.

A lady invited her young unsaved neighbor to this Aglow retreat. She was considering a divorce because her husband did not fulfill her romantic expectations. That weekend she gave her life to Jesus and was gloriously saved.

Before she left the retreat on Sunday I prayed with her and asked God to give her ideas how to love her husband, Joe. I prayed that God would show her how to be fun to live with, without continually preaching at him but rather living the truth she had learned.

Four years later I heard the sequel to this story. She went home and did just what we had prayed about. Joe went to work and the men said, "Joe, what happened to you. You are different!"

"I'll tell you what happened. My wife went to a retreat and came home loving me. Our marriage has changed."

All those men made their wives go to the next Aglow area retreat. When women learn how to operate in the law of the Spirit of life all hell trembles.

The next week, I was speaking for some local Aglow fellowships. I was praying for women at the end of the meeting when a lady walked up to me and slipped a piece of paper into my hand. She said she needed to go home but the Lord had told her to give me this paper. When I was alone I looked at it and it was check for one thousand dollars. No one had ever walked up to me and said the Lord told them to give me a thousand dollars. I knew that this was for the tractor.

We flew home and I called my travel agent for something and she said, "Matilda, are you aware you have money on escrow here?" I couldn't imagine why I should have money in escrow. I later found out that when they would quote a price sometimes it would change by the time they received my payment. Through the years I had built up a credit of $1723. Every cent Wallace needed! It had been filtered to him through his wife, who had thought he really didn't need a tractor. Because she had kept the right attitude, God had used her to bless her husband.

Jason

Our oldest daughter, Carolyn, and her husband Dennis, were expecting their second child. Through an ultrasound they knew it was a boy and so they named him Jason, which means, "Healer."

The morning before his birth, in my morning quiet time, I was reading Psalm 112, especially verses 6-8: "Surely he will never be shaken; a righteous man will be remembered forever. He will have no fear of bad news; his heart is steadfast, trusting in the Lord. His heart is secure, he will have no fear; in the end he will look in triumph on his foes." This scripture so gripped me that I shared it with the family and especially with Carolyn.

The next morning the phone rang and it was Dennis with the news. "We have a 9 lb 1oz baby boy. Everything is fine except for one thing. Jason was born with a cleft lip and palate. The doctor said he is a healthy boy and when the repairs are made we will hardly know it happened."

As I put the phone down tears began to stream down my face. I began to declare the truths God had revealed to me the day before. "My heart is fixed, trusting in you. Light shall arise out of this darkness. How do I know this? Because You are our light and You are our salvation. Our hearts are fixed on You and we will not be moved by these tidings."

I still remember the emotions that I experienced as I looked at this precious child and began to speak truth and life through the hospital window. "Jason, you will not come behind in any good thing. Not in looks, not in intelligence or favor with God and man. Jason, you will be Grandma's mighty man of God. I speak it into your very heart and mind."

God, through a word of prophecy, instructed us to give a good report, so we began to release into this child the Law of the Spirit of life. We would sing and speak the Word of God as we rocked him. Heather, his two-year-old sister, would sing, "There's a miracle in Jason's mouth, hallelujah! There's a miracle in Jason's mouth, hallelujah!" I knew she had learned it from her parents.

When he was three years old, Jason was watching his Daddy play basketball. He looked up at his Mama and said, "I gonna play basketball just like Daddy when I get to be a mighty man of God."

One day he was helping me cut out Christmas cookies and I said, "Jason, God must really love me. I figure God and Jesus were talking one day and they said, 'You know, Grandma Kipfer is traveling all over the world telling people about us. Let's do something very special for her. Why don't we give her Jason as a grandson! We won't give him to just any old grandmother.' You know, Jason, I love you so much that if I knew where to get them, I would get me a dozen more just like you." His little face beamed!

After nine surgeries, my mighty man of God doesn't come behind in any good thing. He is now twenty-four and stands six feet tall. He is an assistant manager at a bank. I wish you could all meet him. You would love his sense of humor and winsome personality. He has a caring heart and recently he helped a woman walk through the trauma of losing her purse. She was so impressed with him that she sent a letter to the manager and also to the newspaper, praising the quality of this young man.

As I have shared the story of Jason, it has ministered deeply to women. We all face challenging situations. Women appreciate knowing the principles of how to walk when the unpredictable occurs. One woman bought the tape of my testimony about Jason and sent it to a missionary couple in Central America, who were walking through the same trial as Carolyn and Dennis. Another woman gave a tape to her doctor and he put it in the library of the Pittsburgh Children's Hospital as one of the resource materials for parents of children facing similar circumstances.

I wish I had understood the Law of life when my children were little. Negative words stop the flow of life. There were blockages in my own life that kept me from giving affirmation to others, so I asked God for ideas. He began to give me simple ideas on how I could give life. You have heard the saying, "An ounce of prevention is worth a pound of cure." The planting of negatives (death) or affirmation (life) will affect your children for a lifetime.

I love grandparenting. It is like a second chance. I have taught my grand- children this little game: First I say, "You are so precious." And they say, "I know it"

"You are a blessing."

"I know it."

"The Spirit of the Lord is poured out on you."

"I know it."

"I am so glad you are mine."

"I know it."

"Grandma is very rich."
    "I know it."
"Why is Grandma rich?"
        "Because you have me!
"How valuable are you?"
        "Worth more than the whole wide world."

One day Amanda, Carolyn's youngest child, was lying on the floor waiting for me to finish at my desk. Out of the blue she said, "Grandma, you are so precious." And I said, "I know it!" I knew Amanda meant every word and it made me feel so good!

As you choose life and give life, it comes back to you. My youngest grandchild is ten years old and my oldest is thirty. I have three great grandchildren, Tirzah, Natilee and Marcus. The girls will often ask me, "Nanna, were you excited when you heard we were coming?" I say, "Yes, I was so excited!"

I want to be a happy memory for my grandchildren and great grandchildren. I want to leave them a legacy of life!

CHAPTER 5

Freedom from the Past: A Revelation of the Cross

Paul in Galatians 6:14-15 concludes his letter with these words: "May I never boast except in the cross of our Lord Jesus Christ, through which the world has been crucified to me, and I to the world. Neither circumcision nor uncircumcision means anything; what counts is a new creation." The hymn writer Isaac Watts wrote:

> When I survey the wondrous cross,
> On which the Prince of glory died,
> My richest gain I count but loss,
> And pour contempt on all my pride.
>
> Forbid it, Lord, that I should boast,
> Save in the death of Christ, my God;
> All the vain things that charm me most,
> I sacrifice them to His blood.
>
> See, from His head, His hands, His feet,
> Sorrow and love flow mingled down;
> Did e'er such love and sorrow meet,
> Or thorns compose so rich a crown?

Were the whole realm of nature mine,
That were a present far too small;
Love so amazing, so divine,
Demands my soul, my life, my all.

The apostle Paul and Issac Watts both received such an understanding of the cross and its meaning that from the point of understanding on, they considered their very lives not their own. Paul most likely wrote his letter to the Philippian church during his first Roman imprisonment in A.D. 61. He was so convinced of the completed work of the cross that even though he was in chains he saw his plight as a chance to advance the Gospel. All the palace guards were touched by his faith and even his Christian brothers were encouraged to speak the word more courageously and fearlessly. This same revelation is what motivated the martyrs to sing as they were burned at the stake. In Philippians 1:21 Paul writes, "For to me, to live is Christ and to die is gain." Even though a part of him wanted to die and be with the Lord, for the sake of the Gospel he was willing to stay.

"Convinced of this, I know that I will remain, and I will continue with all of you for your progress and joy in the faith, so that through my being with you again your joy in Christ Jesus will overflow on account of me. Whatever happens, conduct yourselves in a manner worthy of the gospel of Christ. Then, whether I come and see you or only hear about you in my absence, I will know that you stand firm in one spirit, contending as one man for the faith of the gospel without being frightened in any way by those who oppose you" (Philippians 1:25-28)

The Gospel is good news and I now know that is true. For many years I lived under so many negatives that the message of the cross and my understanding were clouded by guilt, condemnation, and shame. As truth became reality I began to realize that Jesus died for my sins and by receiving Him into my life as Lord of my life, I really have no past. The old self died with Him and is buried with Him, and now I, too, have risen with Christ and the life I now am living I live by the faith of the Son of God who loves me and gave Himself for me. (See Galatians 2:20)

I asked God to give me an illustration that would help people understand this wonderful truth. I thought about modern technology and how we can now record our lives on a video and play it even after we are gone. Suppose Revelation 20:11-15 would read like this: "Then I saw a great white throne and Him who was seated on it. Earth and sky fled from His presence, and there was no place for them. I saw the dead, great and small, standing before the throne. A book was opened, which was the Book of Life. A video began to play revealing every person's entire life. We saw the sea give up its dead, death and hades gave up the dead in them, and each person was judged according to the truth shown in their video. Then came the second death. Death and Hades were thrown into the lake of fire along with anyone whose name was not found in the Lamb's Book Of Life" (paraphrase mine).

In the past this passage struck fear in my heart. We are eternal beings. We have a beginning but we will live forever in either heaven or hell. When the book is opened, everyone will be without excuse. When your life is played it will be absolutely accurate. Every sin committed, every secret thing of the heart, every desire, purpose, or intention will be known. The times we disregarded the sweet disturbances of the Holy Spirit or ignored the opportunities to accept Jesus, all will be flashed before man and all will be without excuse.

The Good News Is This

Salvation is a Person. His name is Jesus. Jesus, the Son of God, became Jesus, the perfect man, the Lamb of God. He offered Himself as a sacrifice. He who had no sin of His own, went to the cross and died for every single past, present, and future sin we ever did or will commit, every wrong desire, every purposeful and intentional sin, and every missed or disregarded opportunity.

"For God so loved the world that he gave his one and only Son, that whoever believes in him shall not perish but have eternal life" (John 3:16).

"Yet to all who received him, to those who believed in his name, he gave the right to become children of God" (John 1:12).

"If we confess our sins, he is faithful and just and will forgive us our sins and purify us from all unrighteousness" (1 John 1:9).

Jesus came to destroy our past video. Once I repent and believe, there is no record of my past sins and they will not follow me into judgment. Since I know this truth, I can now come boldly to His throne and ask for grace whenever I get myself into trouble. It is foolish to try and hide from God when He knows me better than I know myself and there is not anything that is hidden from God.

Those who now believe are making a new video, one where every deed of kindness motivated by Christ's love in us is recorded. A glass of cold water given in His name is like giving it directly to Him. A hug, a smile, a word of encouragement, the dishes I wash with thanksgiving and praise, will all be recorded as good works.

We all miss it at times, but be quick to repent and He will edit them out of your video. Keep right on walking! Romans 5:8-11 says: "But God demonstrates his own love for us in this: While we were still sinners, Christ died for us. Since we have now been justified by his blood, how much more shall we be saved from God's wrath through him! For if, when we were God's enemies, we were reconciled to him through the death of his Son how much more, having been reconciled, shall we be saved through his life! Not only is this so, but we also rejoice in God through our Lord Jesus Christ, through whom we have now received reconciliation."

It's Better to Be a Sheep

In Matthew 25:31-36, Jesus talks about separating the sheep from the goats. When the Son of Man comes and all the holy angels with Him, He will sit on His throne in heavenly glory. All the nations will be gathered before Him and He will separate the people one from another, as a shepherd separates the sheep from the goats. The sheep will be placed on His right and the goats on His left.

"Then the King will say to those on his right, 'Come, you who are blessed by my Father; take your inheritance, the kingdom prepared for you since the creation of the world. For I was hungry and you gave me something to eat, I was thirsty and you gave me something to drink, I was a stranger and you invited me in, I needed clothes and you clothed me, I was sick and you looked after me, I was in prison and you came to visit me'" (Matthew 25:34-36).

The sheep will answer, 'When did we do all that?'

"The King will reply, 'I tell you the truth, whatever you did for one of the least of these brothers of mine, you did for me'" (Matthew 25: 40).

I believe the sheep have truly captured the heart of the shepherd and see needs as opportunities to express His love. The heart of the shepherd is expressed in the church. The natural man is self-absorbed but we now have the heart of the shepherd. We have freely received and we are freely to give this love. Our response to the good news of the Gospel is "ah-ah-amen". Now the goats, on the other hand, are absorbed with themselves. Even though they have heard the good news of the Gospel they have never experienced it for themselves. Their only response is "yes-but". Sometimes I remind the "yes-but" person we all will face the work of the cross, either here in this life or in eternity.

The sheep are not necessarily motivated by needs. The moment we get motivated by needs we try to earn love, but the sheep, seeing needs as opportunities to express God's love, freely respond to their shepherd king by giving themselves to others. They have received so much that they can freely give, not out of obligation, but out of gratitude and love. The sheep realize they are in process. They have a progressive revelation of the cross and refuse to let Jesus' death be in vain in any area of their life.

The goats, being terribly self-absorbed, missed their many opportunities. They talked the walk, but failed when walking the talk. In Matthew 7:21-22 Jesus warns: "Not everyone who says to me, 'Lord, Lord,' will enter the kingdom of heaven, but only he who does the will of my Father who is in heaven. Many will say to me on that day, 'Lord, Lord, did we not prophesy in your name, and in your name drive out demons and perform many miracles?' Then I will tell them plainly, 'I never knew you. Away from me, you evildoers!'"

The "yes-but" Christians live in the past. They say, "I know what the Bible says, but you don't understand. Life has been unfair to me. My past hurts are my life. I wouldn't have anything to talk about; that is who I am. The sin against me was so great, I can't forgive." They cannot see any hope.

It does hurt, but you must realize that you do not need to live out of darkness any longer. Jesus bore that pain. For us to carry this added weight is unnecessary. It is ugly. That is why we react instead of responding with forgiveness. And so for that poor soul, the truth of the matter is that if he doesn't give Jesus his hurts then Jesus' death does not profit him one bit.

We cannot live out of the past. Do you think He forgot you when He said, 'It is finished'? Do you think He should have hung there longer and shed more blood for you? Do you think there wasn't enough blood shed to set you free?

It is time to let go of the past and all the pain that comes with it. Go past your feelings and into the truth of His word. Don't let Him die in vain in any area of your life. That is why Paul could say, "I have wronged no man." The old Saul was now under the blood, so the new Paul could say, "I have wronged no man." He had no past—there was no record.

Effects of a Loud Cry

I used to think when Jesus said, "It is finished," that His voice would have been weak and barely audible. But Mark 15:37 says, "With a loud cry, Jesus breathed His last."

The centurion who stood at the cross heard His cry and saw how He died. And seeing all this he responded with, "Surely, this man was the Son of God."

I believe it came forth so loud and clear that it literally set off an earthquake. Matthew 27:51-53 describes how the earth shook and rocks split. The tombs broke open and bodies of holy people came out of their sepulchers and were seen by many people. The veil of the temple that separated man from God was rent from top to bottom.

Rejoice, Church of God. "IT IS FINISHED!" Jesus, our Savior, hung there long enough. He shed enough blood. We are now free. The old videos are gone and under the blood. Our sins from the past cannot follow us into eternity. We are now, because of the finished work, just as if we had never sinned. We are justified. I had heard it with my ears in the church, over and over again, but now it has become a belt of truth in my life.

I can now stand before Him and accept the fact that I am a child of God and can come boldly to His throne of grace.

New Response to an Old Taunt

When Satan throws the past into my face, and he does, I answer and boldly say, "You've got to be kidding. That's under the blood." I will say, "Flesh, you are not going to get away with this. I will bring you to the light and I will expose you." Remember that the flesh, the unregenerate part of us, is an enemy. The flesh fights the spirit and the spirit fights the flesh. They will never walk side by side. They will never be in fellowship because they are enemies.

Paul writes in Philippians 3:10, "I want to know Christ and the power of his resurrection and the fellowship of sharing in his sufferings, becoming like him in his death."

In verses 12-14, he goes on to say, "Not that I have already obtained all this, or have already been made perfect, but I press on to take hold of that for which Christ Jesus took hold of me. Brothers, I do not consider myself yet to have taken hold of it. But one thing I do: Forgetting what is behind and straining toward what is ahead, I press on toward the goal to win the prize for which God has called me heavenward in Christ Jesus."

When this truth became real to me, I felt so secure in His love that He could now show me that I was the one who needed changing. Before this it was always easier to blame someone else. Now I knew He had hung there long enough and I accepted the responsibility for change.

Past, Present, and Future

One morning during my quiet time, the Holy Spirit asked a question. "Do you understand what your 'life' is?"

"Not really," I answered.

Now you see, my concept of life was the years I had already lived, and my day-to-day living. I had heard an evangelist tell us to come to the altar and give Jesus our lives. I would tell Jesus I was so sorry about the past and would ask Him to forgive me. I would feel good for a few days, but then the enemy would soon come with his accusations and say, "You still think the same way, you still think bad thoughts, and you're still reacting." How many times had I sat in church and sang the words of Fanny Crosby's hymn, "Redeemed how I love to proclaim it! Redeemed by the blood of the Lamb; Redeemed thro' his infinite mercy, His child, and forever, I am." Then I would leave the church feeling guilty and condemned.

I could not grasp the fact that I was a new creation in Christ Jesus. I did not know how to fight the flesh and resist the devil, so therefore I would move into defeat. I felt so bad about the past that I could not enjoy the present. I felt my past had molded my life and that it had ruined my future. You cannot enjoy today when you are worrying about how your life is going to turn out.

That morning the Holy Spirit explained to me, "Your life consists of your past, present, and future. I am the same yesterday, today, and forever. If I am going to be Lord of your life, I need to have your past, all you ever wanted to be and couldn't; all you didn't want to be and were; all of your failures, all of your successes. If you give me your past, I, the Redeemer, will restore the years the locust and cankerworm have eaten. If you will trust me to be Lord, I will release you into creative living. I will give you ideas to build your house. I want you to be free and not waste your time vindicating yourself. I will do that. It is not your job to change, convert, or save anyone. Let me change you, and then I will use you to change your family, your church, and even the world."

The truth of this revelation has forever changed my approach to God. I dropped the thee's and the thou's and He truly became "Abba, Father", a dear Papa to me. This radically changed my life. I understood now why Paul said, "I glory in the cross of Jesus Christ."

"Father, I pray that the 'It is finished' will be so loud in all of our lives that every bondage and chain is broken. I pray beauty, joy, and praise to come forth like a mighty river. I pray the revelation of the accomplished work of the cross becomes so real and practical in our lives that the world will get saved. I thank you that the Gospel is good news. Whether we live or whether we die we belong to Jesus. Therefore, we will not allow offenses or unforgiveness, the hurts of life or resentment, or any other work of the flesh to hinder our relationship with Jesus. I will choose You Jesus, over having my own way, fighting for my rights, or feeling sorry for myself. I know that you live in my heart, therefore I can speak forth with my mouth that which I believe and that is: I am free from the past, free to enjoy today, and free to enjoy the tomorrows that I have not even seen. Thank you, Lord."

I know the blood will never lose its power. When memories surface I can now praise God. I have a little saying that goes like this: "What I do know is so much more powerful than what I don't know. If I never know what I don't know, it really doesn't matter. If I operate in what I do know, it puts me over every single time." I know that He will never give me back what He has put under the blood. It is buried in the sea of His forgetfulness. Memories are now reminders to give thanks. I can't squeeze an ounce of inspiration out of the hurts of life. That is why Jesus died. I am now free to operate in life and not death. I choose life!

Paul and Silas understood the work of the cross. With their feet in stocks and backs bleeding they sang and praised God. Around midnight, as the prisoners were listening to them, suddenly a great earthquake shook the prison house. The doors opened and chains fell off. The jailer was about to kill himself, thinking all the prisoners had escaped but instead Paul preached the Gospel to him and he and all his household were saved. He washed Paul and Silas' wounds, fed them, and rejoiced greatly because he now believed (Acts 16:22-36).

The revelation of the cross still sets off earthquakes. It releases such power that the chains of the past fall off. The wounds are healed. The prisoners and jailers of the world are still being set free. In restricted countries where there is a high price for salvation, the prisoners still are being set free.

We can now walk in the understanding that our past is under the blood. Yesterday is gone, tomorrow may never be ours, but today is the day the Lord has given us. We can enjoy today, because He is the Lord of our past, present and future. "May I never boast except in the cross of our Lord Jesus Christ, through which the world has been crucified to me, and I to the world" (Galatians 6:14).

I tried for years to earn my salvation through good behavior. I thought if I obeyed all the rules God would be pleased with me. Instead I found no peace or rest until like Paul, I saw the cross clearly.

Eugene Peterson says it so beautifully in Colossians 3:12-17 in *The Message*: "So, chosen by God for this new life of love, dress in the wardrobe God picked out for you: compassion, kindness, humility, quiet strength, discipline. Be even-tempered, content with second place, quick to forgive an offense. Forgive as quickly and completely as the Master forgave you. And regardless of what else you put on, wear love. It's your basic, all-purpose garment. Never be without it.

"Let the peace of Christ keep you in tune with each other, in step with each other. None of this going off and doing your own thing. And cultivate thankfulness. Let the Word of Christ—the Message—have the run of the house. Give it plenty of room in your lives. Instruct and direct one another using good common sense. And sing, sing your hearts out to God! Let every detail in your lives—words, actions, whatever—be done in the name of the Master, Jesus, thanking God the Father every step of the way."

CHAPTER 6

Helping Your Children Find Their Way

Proverbs 22:6 instructs us to "train a child in the way he should go, and when he is old he will not turn from it." Training children in the way they should go means the way God intended them to go, following His plans for their lives, and not living a parent's dreams or desires.

I understood well the pain of living out a life that you may not have been destined for. Wallace had never wanted to farm but felt forced to carry out his father's dream. He wasn't given a choice as he grew into manhood, and back when we grew up it was just understood that sons continue in their father's profession. So as we raised our children we tried to encourage their natural giftings.

Whenever the children would play church, Galen was always the pastor. He would preach with real gusto. Eventually he became a pastor.

Carolyn would go to the library and bring home books on doctors and nurses. She rarely missed Dr. Kildare on the television and today she is a nurse.

Don had a yen to fly. When he was about five or six, he tried it! He caught two chickens, and with a chicken in each hand, he climbed up on the hen house roof, held on to their legs, and jumped. His flight was short-lived and the landing rough, but it did not alter his course. Today he flies 747 cargo planes all over the world.

Mary Jane gravitated to the piano. She would pound out songs and she wasn't very old when she began to compose her own music. Today she still sings, writes music, and is asked to come and lead worship at meetings and conferences all around the United States.

Wallace and I may not have always agreed with all of their decisions but we honored their right to hear from God as individuals. So when Galen and Debbie came home and said, "We believe that God is asking us to quit our jobs and start working full time at the *Coffee House*," I would not be truthful if I did not say that Wallace and I were a bit concerned. They went on to say, "This is between God and us. It will be a walk of faith. We have either heard from God or we have not."

Then Mary Jane said, "Mom and Dad, I feel God is telling me to go to Youth With a Mission instead of to college to study music." A few days later she said, "Mom and Dad, I think the Lord is asking me to give all my savings to a pastor and his family. I am still going to Youth With A Mission, though. I don't want you to pick up the care. It is between God and me."

And then our son Don came to us and said, "Mom and Dad, I could do construction work all my life and get by, but it's not what I would like to do. I want to fly." Then a few nights later he said, "Mom and Dad, I quit my job. I am going to college to be a pilot." We felt stretched!

The only one who seemed normal at the time was Carolyn. She had graduated from college and married a wonderful man named Dennis from Oregon. They were both employed, happily married, and living in Virginia.

Now what did I say earlier about allowing them to express their God given giftings…

Providence

Galen and Debbie needed a new car because their Volvo barely ran. Our pastor also needed a new van. Galen and Debbie decided to start a van fund for him, so they took their car money, seeded the fund, and encouraged everyone to participate. Meanwhile Galen needed to pray just to get the Volvo started.

Galen would confidently say, "Wait until you see our new one." Even his three-year-old daughter, Gretchen would say, "Grandma, we have a new car."

I would say, "You do, where is it?"

"It is still in the garage," she would reply.

But there came a time when no matter how much we prophesied over that dry Volvo, it died, never to go again, and they had to use our car.

One day I heard horns blowing. I looked out the window and saw a new '88 Oldsmobile coming up the driveway, followed by our Chevy. I can still see Gretchen's little face all lit up as she said, "I told you Grandma, we have a new car!" Someone had given them a car, all expenses paid.

Gretchen learned to trust God at a very young age. One morning she was tired of cereal and wanted eggs for breakfast. She began to whine.

"Gretchen, how do we get eggs?" asked her mom.

"We ask Jesus with a thankful heart and praise Him," she answered. Now it just so happened that a man from the church had chickens. As he drove past the *Coffee House* that morning, the Lord spoke to him and said, "Go back and get eggs for Galen and Debbie."

While they were praising the Lord the doorbell rang, and there were Gretchen's eggs! Her little faith soared when she saw how quickly God had answered her prayer. Building on her breakfast experience, she said to her mother, "Be sure to get puppy food when you go to the store. I have prayed for a puppy."

Debbie smiled and didn't take Gretchen's request seriously. Later that evening the doorbell rang and when Debbie answered, there it was: a lively, little puppy tied to the doorknob.

Mary Jane

Meanwhile, Mary Jane continued working at the department store and at home was making macramé to sell. When she was asked about her future plans, she would say with assurance, "I'm going to Youth With a Mission."

Others would ask me the same question and I would say hesitantly, "She is planning to go to Youth With a Mission."

One day the Lord said, "You could at least agree with her." So I began trying to say more positively, "She is going to Youth With a Mission." She had earned enough for her plane ticket and the down payment for her trip but still needed one thousand dollars.

A Mother's SOS

It was December and because snow was predicted I was outdoors pushing the leaves from our yard to the edge of the cornfield. As I worked I was praying. "We have laid our lives on the line for you, Lord. Galen and Debbie are believing you for today's bread. Don is on a venture of faith in college and flight school. Mary Jane needs one thousand dollars for the YWAM trip in January and we simply don't have it."

The next morning I went to our monthly Aglow meeting. Barbara, a woman who had been attending the Wednesday morning Bible study at the coffee house walked up to me and asked, "Matilda, were you looking for money yesterday morning?"

"Why do you ask?" I responded

"The Lord showed me you were searching through envelopes and I asked him, 'What is she looking for?'"

"Money!" He replied.

"How much does she need?"

"One thousand dollars."

The following Wednesday morning Barbara shared our conversation with the Bible study group. She came up with an idea to raise money for Mary Jane. She asked if anyone would like to donate items for a sale. Barbara, being an antique dealer, suggested they bring in an antique.

When we arrived at the coffee house and saw the valuable items that had been donated, we were so overcome by the extravagant love that had motivated such generosity, that we wept. The sale brought in all but two hundred dollars but not all the items were sold that day.

The day before Mary Jane left, she needed to get her money

changed into an international check before the bank closed at 3:00 in the afternoon. She still needed the two hundred dollars. I had seen so many miracles that I knew God would not let us down now. I looked at her and said, "It will be here."

At noon, a friend came with fifty dollars. At 2:00 in the afternoon another precious lady brought three hundred dollars. Mary Jane left for Youth With a Mission the following morning.

On Her Way

As money from the sale of the remaining antiques came in we would send it to Mary Jane. We knew that she would now have enough for her entire trip so imagine our surprise when we received a letter saying, "Mom and Dad, I need to tell you that I gave my money away to people who did not yet have all their money for the first phase of the program. Those of us who needed money for our upcoming field trip wrote our names on the blackboard tonight and we prayed. I need to get to bed because we leave early tomorrow morning. Love, Mary Jane. P.S. We are on our way. I went down and looked on the board and by my name was written, 'Paid in full.' Must go!"

Letters from Mary Jane always brought excitement to the house. We missed her but we knew she was doing what the Lord wanted and she was happy.

One day Carolyn stopped in as I was reading one of her letters. I started reading the letter to her aloud and came to a section that read, "Lord, I am willing to stay single the rest of my life. But I ask to be so in love with you that it doesn't matter if I ever get married." Carolyn, who thought that married life was next to heaven blurted out, "Mom, that's awful."

Surprise at Christmas

It was Christmas and Mary Jane had been gone for nearly a year. Our whole family, except Don, used our pastor's van to go to Kennedy Airport to pick her up. We were so excited to see her.

We left the airport and stopped to fill the gas tank for the long

trek back to western New York. Wallace, Mary Jane, and I were in
the back seat. Debbie and Carolyn were seated in the middle with
Galen and Dennis in the driver's seats. The lights from the station
were shining in the van windows so I could clearly see Mary Jane's
face. We knew for sometime that she had something special to tell
us which could not be written in a letter. One of the leaders had
encouraged Mary Jane to cut a record of the songs God had given
her over the years and Wallace and I were sure she was going to
surprise us with an album for Christmas. As I looked at her I asked
her, "Where do we begin?"

"You need to ask me some questions." Mary Jane replied.

"As a starter, what was it you were going to tell us but could not
write in a letter?"

"I don't think we should start there." she said

Carolyn looked right at her and said, "You're getting married,
aren't you!"

I thought W*hat a ridiculous thing to say* but when I looked at
Mary Jane's face, I knew it was true. I managed to ask, "Mary Jane
is that true?"

"Yes."

"To whom?"

She had written about a young man from California, but had
insisted he was just a good friend. His name flashed before me.
Then I heard her say, "His name is Derek Bevan and he is from
Belfast, Ireland."

A dreadful silence came into the van. Wallace lost his speech
along with all the rest of us. I had so wanted this time to be a perfect
memory and now no one knew what to say. I tried to explain that no
one was talking because we were in shock. It felt like a stranger had
come into our family and was taking our daughter.

In YWAM serious relationships are discouraged. The teams live
in the same house, eat together, and minister together. If two people
begin to be attracted to one another they are encouraged to go to the
leadership for counsel. After she had prayed her prayer of surrender
and was willing to remain single all her life, she did experience a
wonderful love relationship with the Lord. But she also began to
have feelings for Derek. She went to the leadership and shared her

feelings. Bill and Jean Davidson, who were leaders at the time, knew both Mary Jane and Derek and were delighted with the possibility that God might be putting these two together. Bill was like a father to Derek and thought highly of Mary Jane. He began telling Derek that there was a young woman who felt he was a very special person. He gave enough hints so that Derek soon figured out who it was and was relieved that it was Mary Jane.

No one on the team had ever guessed they were falling in love. Derek never expressed his feelings for her. It was just something they both felt when they were together. Two nights before she was to fly home for Christmas he asked her to marry him. Later, when I went back through her letters, sure enough, Derek's name came up quite often.

Her brothers were very protective of her. Don felt that her songs and music were good enough to open doors for a professional career and if she got married and had children, she would never cut her album. Galen had reservations right up until the wedding day. And Wallace, my dear Wallace, was struggling as only a loving father could.

But Mary Jane had heard from God, and Derek, without a shadow of a doubt was the man that God had provided for her.

Our Pilot

Don finished school and now was a pilot. He applied for many different jobs but the one he really wanted was flying Lear jets for Carborundum, in Niagara Falls. He had become friends with one of their pilots, Tom who was a Christian, but nothing seemed to be working out for Don.

One night he came home so discouraged. I took one look at him and ran downstairs to the laundry room, which had become my prayer closet. As I was praying, Psalm 86 came to mind. It starts out by saying, "Hear, O Lord, and answer me, for I am poor and needy." I kept on reading and when I got to verse 15, I found my *rhema* word. "But you, O Lord, are a compassionate and gracious God, slow to anger, abounding in love and faithfulness. Turn to me and have mercy on me; grant your strength to your servant and save the son of your maidservant. Give me a sign of your goodness, that my enemies may see it and be put to shame, for you, O Lord, have helped me and comforted me." I began to rejoice! Yes, Lord give me a sign.

At 8:00 that evening the phone rang. It was the Heussler Company asking Don if he would like a job flying a twin engine plane that they had just purchased. I heard Don answer, "I sure do!" They informed him they would contact him in about a week when the plane arrived and they needed him to come in and be measured for a uniform.

By the end of the week no call had come and again discouragement set in. Down I went to my "prayer closet laundry room". "Now Lord, I know you don't dangle something in front of our faces and then pull it out of our reach. I am asking for another sign."

At 10:00 that night Carborundum called and asked Don if he would like a job. Don was elated but he dreaded having to call Heusslers and tell them he was going to choose Carborundum. When he finally called he found the deal had fallen through and there was no plane. No one there had the courage to call and tell him.

A few days later Heusslers called back. They had the plane now and asked him if he was still interested in the job. Don explained about the job offer with Carborundum. The man on the other end of the line said he would be a fool to take their job over Carborundum. He, himself, had been trying to get hired by Carborundum for years.

Thank-you Father, You are so good and faithful and so ever present to show Yourself strong on our behalf.

Moving In and Out

All of our children were once again living near us and grand-children were coming along. I sensed that this was going to be a short season for us and I wanted to use this time to create happy memories.

Our family did soon start to scatter. Don moved to Houston, Texas, where he met Carol. They now live in Anchorage, Alaska along with our grandson, Austin.

Derek, Mary Jane, and their two children, Peter, and Jenny

moved to upstate New York. Derek became a pastor of a church and their youngest child, Chad, was born.

In 1986 we sold our farm and moved to Arizona. Five years later, due to property that did not sell, we moved back to Lake Luzerne ourselves where we still live today and Derek is now our pastor.

Dennis, Carolyn, Heather, Jason, and Amanda moved to Portland, Oregon where they still live today.

Galen, Debbie, and their children, Gretchen, Abby, and Josh moved to Lake Luzerne, New York.

Yes, it can be a trying role allowing our young adult children to find their way. It can be challenging, delightful, and heartbreaking, but also filled with joy. It is a time of hoping, believing, praying, and releasing. It is a whole new walk with God. When our children marry, the role of being the parent changes and becomes a supporting role. They need to learn from their successes and failures just like we did. We would like to spare them from the heartaches and the disappointments of life, but we need to allow them to experience these in order to have the growth and satisfaction that come from working through the hard places.

So the ducklings continue quacking and the goslings keep flying north or wherever. And this old goose and gander just keep staying the course.

The family when they were young: (left to right) Galen, Ray, Carolyn Joyce, Mary Jane, Donald Wayne.

Our Wedding

CHAPTER 7

Women on the Move

"Could I speak to Matilda Kipfer please?"
"This is she speaking."

"Matilda, I'm Mary Weirich, president of the Buffalo Women's Aglow chapter. Your name was give to us as a potential board member. We are having a board meeting and could you come?"

I said I would be there. I had heard Aglow mentioned now and then and had wondered about the group so I thought it would be good to check it out. I had heard it was an interdenominational international Christian women's organization, based out of Seattle, Washington.

I arrived at the house and John Garlington, a friend of ours and also an adviser for the Aglow ministry, put out his hand and said, "Welcome to Women's Aglow, Matilda!"

I thought *What a pleasant welcome!* But as the day went on I began to wonder if they already thought I was on the board. I left that day shaking my head and when I arrived home I said to Wallace, "I'm not sure, but I think I'm on the board of the Buffalo Women's Aglow."

In 1974 my name was added to the board. Now this is not the usual way you join an organization. Usually you check out the doctrinal beliefs first and if you agree with them, then you join. God does have a sense of humor and knowing my tendency to underestimate my ability, He gave me a big shove and pushed me in. Eventually I became President of the Buffalo Chapter and the Area Board President. From there I went on to become a field representative. I also served on the International Board for many years.

Shortly after that I had a dream. In the dream I was speaking to a large crowd. I was not a woman who was given to dreams and their meanings but this was different. I felt God was speaking to me.

A few months later Mary asked if I would share my testimony at the next month's meeting. I said, "Sure, I can do that." There was a group of Baptist ladies there that night and they invited me to come and speak for their women, I said, "Sure, I can do that." God honored His word as I followed His leading. I realized I could do anything God asked of me if I was willing to do it with my unique personality and His ability. I really can't remember what happened next. I just know I bought a little date book and started to keep track of all the speaking invitations that began coming in.

I released the Wednesday morning Bible study to my good friend, Varona Danner, whom I had mentored. I soon found myself a full-time Aglow woman. Wallace was working and could not drive me around. I was not a good navigator and began to move out of my comfort zone. We only had one car so I said to Wallace, "I have never done this before but if you let me buy a car, I believe God will supply all the money needed for this car." So we bought a brand new little gray Omni with a sharp red interior. It became my prayer closet. God taught me many things in that little car.

This was so opposite to what I thought that I would be doing, that I asked the Lord to give me three confirmations like He did for Gideon, so I would know this truly was God calling me. First, I asked that my husband would have twice as strong a confirmation as I had. The assignment God had given me was against everything Wallace and I had been taught. It was all right for men to travel without their wives but not the other way around.

Second, I asked that I would be able to sleep away from home. I had trouble sleeping at home much less away from home. I can now sleep on planes, in airports and in strange beds.

Third, since I had no sense of direction and I needed to travel by myself, I needed help big time! With the directions in my left hand, the Lord and I found our way through towns, villages, and eventually, through cities.

Evelyn Steele, our regional director for the northwest New England states, suggested that I fly. "No one will ever pay for my airfare," I quickly responded. As I thought about this I decided perhaps that would help me control all the invitations that were coming my way. The next time I received a call I very gingerly said, "I would be delighted to come but I would need to fly." To my utter surprise I heard, "No problem, we will send you the ticket."

It was on a flight home from Pittsburgh, as I checked in my little date book to see the next week's agenda, that I realized my life had changed forever. I believe God had put blinders on me until I had enough truth in me to handle a fraction of what He saw. If He could work out all this, I could also trust Him to help my husband embrace the changes this was bringing into our family and marriage.

Walking Through the Valley

Wallace and I were not used to being apart and this brought tension into our marriage. As we were on our way to the Buffalo airport one morning, I could tell Wallace was struggling. He was very quiet and I tried to get him to share what was bothering him but he wouldn't talk. I asked him if he thought that my assignment was over. He said he didn't think so and that he would work through whatever this was that was bothering him.

The tension between us became so great that at times I felt I could hardly breathe. The valley between Wallace's verbal consent and his heart where he was hurting seemed impassable. In this valley we deal with feelings and by faith we walk through this valley. In Romans 10:10 we read, "For it is with your heart that you believe and are justified, and it is with your mouth that you confess and are saved." Eugene Peterson in *The Message* words it this way, "The word that saves is right here, as near as the tongue in your mouth, as close as the heart in your chest."

Out of our hearts comes righteousness and with our mouths we confess what we believe. The in-between is our feelings. We must walk with truth in our hearts and we must confess the truth with our mouths. By faith we will walk out our salvation.

"Therefore, my dear friends, as you have always obeyed—not only in my presence, but now much more in my absence—continue to work out your salvation with fear and trembling, for it is God who works in you to will and to act according to his good purpose" (Philippians 2:12-13).

Each one of us must walk through this valley with God alone. I had often wondered why God had given me such a dramatic call but I now know that it was for times like this, when I would feel that I could not go on.

As I sat there beside this man that I loved feeling as though I were suffocating, I desperately prayed, "Lord, I know that this assignment was never my idea, but perhaps you are through with it and I am still locked in. I need another big confirmation. I want one so big I could never miss it."

I flew to North Carolina. The Aglow girls had a lunch for all the board members and ministry chairmen. As I walked into the house two ladies became extremely excited. One of them, Jo Ann Cox had received a vision eighteen months earlier. She saw a woman and the Lord said to her that He was going to use this woman to bless many women and she also, would be blessed by her and to pray for her daily.

Her mother also had a dream. In the dream she saw a woman on television and was given the same message; she was to pray for this woman. As these two women shared with each other they came to the conclusion that it had to be the same woman. So they began to pray and watch for what God was going to do. When I walked into the room, I was the woman they had both seen. That was a big enough confirmation for me! Thank you Lord, I could not miss that!

Four years later I again was asking for a confirmation. It is possible to get so locked into the old that we can miss the new place God wants to open for us. I had just finished a retreat in North Dakota. I was to fly out Sunday morning but before I left, the Aglow ladies wondered if I would like to go to the opening night of a citywide tent meeting. We went and while there I was called forward by a man I had never seen or even heard of.

"You have been asking God for a confirmation, haven't you?"

"Yes, Sir, I have." I replied. He began to prophesy that I have only seen a tip of what God is planning to do through me and God would open up the waters and send me to the nations. As of today, I have spoken in thirteen different countries.

We need to remember that we are all very ordinary with an extraordinary God who does extraordinary things in us and through us. I am grateful to God for allowing me to serve side by side with my Aglow sisters around the world.

A Call To Prayer

As in Jeremiah 9:17-21, God is again calling women to direct their sensitivity towards heaven and pray for our homes, churches, nations, and the world.

"The Lord of Hosts says: Send for the mourners! Quick! Begin your crying! Let the tears flow from your eyes. Hear Jerusalem weeping in despair. 'We are ruined! Disaster has befallen us! We must leave our land and homes!' Listen to the words of God, O women who wail. Teach your daughters to wail and your neighbors too. For death has crept through your window into your homes. He has killed off the flower of your youth. Children no longer play in the streets; the young men gather no more in the squares." (Living Bible)

This sounds like today's evening news. We must not retreat or live in fear. The church must begin to pray. *Prayer is the most powerful way to release the ministry of Jesus into this perishing world.*

"The wise woman builds her house, but with her own hands the foolish one tears hers down." (Proverbs 14:1)

The call and the responsibility to pray is essential for our homes. We, as women, wives, mothers, or grandmothers, through our diligence in prayer, have begun to turn back the tide of evil and turn men's hearts again towards their families.

I praise God that the Aglow Ministry has stressed the importance of prayer. This ministry has now connected women with women of all nations and all tongues. God has put into place an army of praying women and only he can orchestrate that for His ultimate glory and purpose. As our prayers blend together and flow towards the throne of God, the bowls of heaven are filled with our petitions and God then begins to pour out His blessings on this earth.

Women! If ever there has been a time to pray it is now! The future of our nations, our families, and our churches balances on the power of our prayers. I am not a woman who is prone to the dramatic, but I do know this, the earth is beginning to be shaken. The time is not some far off future; the time is now.

God's Provision and Love

Women will come up to me and say how wonderful it must be to travel and to meet new and interesting people. God has blessed me greatly. I have never lost my luggage or missed a meeting because of illness or travel problems. But to be quite honest, doing the will of God has its lonely times and not only for myself but for my husband as well. Not many men in the church know how to encourage a man whose wife is gone every weekend during the busy retreat months. Wallace often hears remarks like, "Where is she off to this weekend?" Or "Wally, can't you keep her at home!" "I have a word from the Lord for you, Wally. Your wife is to stay home and take care of your needs."

Words can be so hurtful even if meant in fun. "The tongue has the power of life and death, and those who love it will eat its fruit." (Proverbs 18:21)

I may have been flying high in the sky but emotionally I was very low and lonely. Wallace had shared his heart the night before with our prayer and share group about some of the struggles he was experiencing. I knew that I was the cause of his pain, but my choice was either I disobey God and stay at home or I continue on and let God deal with Wallace. I couldn't fix it for Wally. Our pastor agreed that I needed to keep doing what God had called me to do, or else I would hinder the work God was doing in my husband and myself.

I began to treat every invitation as an open door and I knew that as I walked towards it I could trust him to close every door that was not His.

God had spoken to my heart and said, "If you will dare to be my unique woman I will uniquely use you. If you stay in my rest I will cause people to be astounded at what I will do through you."

It is easy to become distracted by the opposition's forces. But if we remember greater is He that is in you than he that is in the world and if God truly calls us, He *will* equip us for the assignment. We often waste precious time defending ourselves and forget that God is our vindicator. If we want to reign with Him, we also need to suffer with Him.

The next morning, as I was flying, I turned my face to the window so no one could see my tears. As I looked out the window the Lord reminded me that the clouds of our lives will never stop the "sonshine" of His love for us. I wiped my tears and reached for the Delta airlines magazine in the pocket of the seat in front of me. I opened it and randomly glanced through it and to my surprise found a full page copy of the poem, "Footprints."

It was beautifully written on paper bordered by flowers. I knew it was God again saying, "I called you and I will carry you when you feel too weak to walk." I thanked Him for that tap on my shoulder and I knew I could keep walking.

I really wanted that complimentary copy to take with me. I had plans to frame it. I was already off the plane when I remembered I had left it on the seat beside of me. I decided it wasn't that important and besides I was coming back within a few days so I would be sure to get a copy then.

Before the retreat started, a pastor came and gave me a bookmark. He felt that he was to give it to me and that I would know why. It had the poem "Footprints" on the front. Before the retreat ended a woman who had never met me or heard any of my teaching tapes, handed me a gift-wrapped package. She was on her way out of the Christian bookstore and felt the Lord spoke to her and said, "I want you to buy this for Matilda Kipfer. She will know why."

It was a wall plaque with the same poem, "Footprints" written on it. Today it hangs in our bedroom where I can easily be reminded of His provision and love.

On my flight back, I could not find the poem in any of the magazines. I even pulled the pages apart to see if anyone had torn it out. I looked in at least three or four and it simply was not there. I began to realize there had only been one copy and it had been divinely put there just for me.

"Footprints" came to our house in greeting cards and even Christmas cards that year. I am so grateful for all the love notes He sends in our lifetime. "How great is the love the father has lavished on us that we should be called, children of God." That is just who we are, His children.

Look for His love notes in every sunrise and sunset, the majestic mountains and the bubbling streams, the variety of plant life and animals and birds. Every newborn baby has His signature. Those little "coincidences" that happen daily, I call love taps. Jesus is letting us know, "Fear not little flock because in the hard places I will carry you..."

Thank you....

I would like to give honor to all the pastors who see the ministry of Aglow as God ordained and who are willing to stand with us in an advisory position. They are faithful men who through the years have seen the will and the purposes of God in this woman-to-woman ministry.

Evelyn Steele, who was National Director of the Northeast Quadrant and Bette Davis, who was the Area President for New York State at the time I became involved in Aglow, modeled the ministry of Aglow in such a way that I felt privileged to be a part of it. They saw potential in me that I could not see. Then there was Jane Hansen and Sharon Barrett. These women are only a few of the many women that God used mightily in my life. I have been honored to have served on the local, area, national, and international boards with women of integrity and dedication. As I sat under their leadership and their leadership training they drew out of me the giftings and purposes of God and for this I say, "Thank-you!"

CHAPTER 8

Mentoring in Every Season

As I became actively involved in the Aglow ministry I knew unless we were preparing young women to fill our places, the future of this ministry would have a limited number of years. I had a great desire to see younger women have the same opportunities to serve that I had experienced.

For years the Lord had laid it on my heart to pray for my successor. I was content with serving on the National and International Boards but I felt God was telling me it was time for a change. It would have been easier to stay with the familiar, but God's timing and His will were what I sought. When I was asked to continue on the Aglow International Board for another three years I said I would with the stipulation that when my successor arrived, I could be released.

In 1996, at the International Conference, I was sitting beside Janet McGee at an Intercultural Committee meeting when suddenly I knew she was the woman who would replace me. Yet, as I looked across the room I saw another woman, Delores Moore, who I also felt was the woman who would replace me. What was going on?

It was not until later, at the Rhode Island National Conference, it occurred to me that I had served on two boards, the National and the International. Janet is now serving on the National Board and Delores is on the International. God had given my assignment to two women instead of just one.

That night I went to my bed and wept. The friendships I had forged would be for an eternity, but I would miss the contact with these wonderful women. Although the change was painful, I knew that I was in God's will and that it was time to move over. God had shown me that I was not stepping down. In fact, we never step down when we are doing the will of God, we just move over. That moving over provides a space for the next person to step into as we continue to march shoulder to shoulder in the army of God.

Later, when I arrived home after the conference, I had my first invitation to come to China. Many times I have wondered if that invitation would have been offered to me if I had not been obedient in relinquishing my position.

What Kind of Love. . . . .

With this new adventure came a greater desire to know Jesus more. I began finding that to know Him is to love Him. The more I loved Him, the more I wanted to serve Him and serving Him was an unmerited privilege. God cannot help Himself, He is love! This extravagant love must be expressed. His eyes run to and fro over the earth looking for pure hearts to pour His love into.

For God so *loved* the world that he *gave* his only begotten son, His absolute best. What kind of love is this that He, Jesus, would lay aside His heavenly body and come to earth as a baby, even to be born in a barn. If video libraries are in heaven this is the first one I want played.

"Who, although being essentially one with God and in the form of God (possessing the fullness of the attributes which make God God), did not think this equality with God was a thing to be eagerly grasped or retained,

But stripped Himself (of all privileges and rightful dignity), so as to assume the guise of a servant (slave), in that He became like men and was born a human being.

And after He had appeared in human form, He abased and humbled Himself (still further) and carried His obedience to the extreme of death, even the death of the cross!" (Philippians 2:6-8 AMP)

What kind of love is this, that opened the way for Jesus to strip Himself of the form of God and also God's attributes and strip Himself of all the privileges and His rightful dignity, so as to become a man, a common man? What kind of love enabled Him to do this?

Eugene Peterson explains it like this: "Think of yourselves the way Christ Jesus thought of himself. He had equal status with God but didn't think so much of himself that he had to cling to the advantages of that status no matter what. Not at all. When the time came, he set aside the privileges of deity and took on the status of a slave, became human! Having become human, he stayed human. It was an incredibly humbling process. He didn't claim special privileges. Instead, he lived a selfless, obedient life and then died a selfless, obedient death—and the worst kind of death at that: a crucifixion."

My mind cannot fathom this type of love. I humbly bow before this man Jesus, who chose this for the likes of me. He chose forever to be identified with man and even today is sitting at the right hand of the Father, representing the sons of man, defending us. And we, by the power of His Spirit, are the sons of God, representing Him on the earth.

We will always be able to recognize Him because He will have nail scarred hands and feet. Again, why did He do this? Isaiah 61:1-3 describes his purpose like this, "The Spirit of the Sovereign Lord is on me, because the Lord has anointed me to preach good news to the poor.

He has sent me to bind up the brokenhearted, to proclaim freedom for the captives and release from darkness for the prisoners, to proclaim the year of the Lord's favor and the day of vengeance of our God, to comfort all who mourn, and provide for those who grieve in Zion—to bestow on them a crown of beauty instead of ashes, the oil of gladness instead of mourning, and a garment of praise instead of a spirit of despair. They will be called oaks of righteousness, a planting of the Lord for the display of his splendor."

This is about ordinary people, like you and I, showing the world what God is like. He did this so we could know His Father, our Father. His ministry is still the same, to know God and to make Him known throughout the world through His church, which is His body.

Mary the Young

One December I was teaching the Christmas story, when God gave me a revelation of three women so in love with God that he used them to change the world. I love the story of Christmas. It is one of the greatest love stories ever written and chapters of that story continue to be written today, using your life and mine. We are to be living epistles, known and read by all men.

Mary was anywhere from thirteen to fifteen years of age. She lived under Roman rule and well understood about oppression. She was well acquainted with the scriptures for she knew of the promised Messiah. She was engaged to be married to Joseph, a carpenter. I can just picture her daydreaming of her future as a wife and a mother. In the midst of this, an angel, named Gabriel, appeared to Mary and gave her such an assignment that if Mary had not known and loved God, it would have been impossible to comprehend. It defied all human reasoning and explanation. The more mature would have said, "She is too young for such an important assignment. The salvation of the world resting on a teenager, never! That cannot possibly be God. This job requires someone with maturity."

But I ask you again, what kind of love are we talking about here? This love enabled her to embrace an assignment that would rattle her world and bring about criticism, rejection and possibly even death. This was love so beyond human understanding that she could answer with, "May it be to me as you have said."

Luke 1:38 ends with these words, "Then the angel left her." Now it is one thing to have an angel in your presence, but quite another to be standing alone with no witnesses to fall back on as you share some earthshaking news. "I am pregnant. No, it is not Joseph's child, it is God's." What must it have been like for her family and fiancé? The law said, "Stone such a woman." The unbelievable shock to their emotions can only be imagined. *There is one thing we can be sure of: God will take care of the many people who are affected by the call or assignment on our lives.* Matthew 1:19-20 gives us a peek into this: "Because Joseph her husband was a righteous man and did not want to expose her to public disgrace, he had in mind to divorce her quietly. But after he had considered this, an angel appeared to him in a dream and said, 'Joseph, Son of David, do not be afraid to take Mary home as your wife.'"

God took care of her Joseph. Do we believe He will take care of our "Josephs" as well?

Elizabeth the Middle-Aged

I am so glad there was one woman in Mary's life who could appreciate a miracle. All the relatives knew Elizabeth was barren and past the childbearing years. It does not give us her age but we know she had experienced the changes of middle life and bore the disappointment and shame of being childless. Now Gabriel came to her husband Zechariah the priest and gave him the news that Elizabeth was going to have a very special baby. His name was to be John and he would be great in the sight of the Lord. His response to the angel was, "'How can I be sure of this? I am an old man and my wife is well along in years.' The angel answered, 'I am Gabriel. I stand in the presence of God, and I have been sent to speak to you and to tell you this good news. And now you will be silent and not able to speak until the day this happens, because you did not believe my words, which will come true at their proper time'" (Luke 1:18-20). Thus, because of his unbelief, Zechariah had to relay all this information to his wife by making signs for he could not talk until his son was born.

Elizabeth was in her sixth month of pregnancy. Imagine if you will, the setting of this moment in history when Elizabeth greets Mary. She opens the door and outside stands a young, unmarried, and pregnant relative with a child more precious then Elizabeth's own. There is no doubt about it, this was a woman who knew her God and had a heart after Him. Her words of welcome were… "Blessed are you among women, and blessed is the child you will bear! But why am I so favored, that the mother of my Lord should come to me? As soon as the sound of your greeting reached my ears, the baby in my womb leaped for joy. Blessed is she who has believed that what the Lord has said to her will be accomplished!" (Luke 1:42-45)

I want to love God so completely that I will be able to see the purposes of God in the young as well. Elizabeth's words of encouragement, belief and acceptance drew a song out of Mary. We need to remember that Mary sang this song *before* she knew God had spoken to her Joseph. It was an incredible song of worship and praise!

"And Mary said: 'My soul glorifies the Lord and my spirit rejoices in God my Savior,

For he has been mindful of the humble state of his servant.

From now on all generations will call me blessed,

For the Mighty One has done great things for me—Holy is his name.

His mercy extends to those who fear him, from generation to generation.

He has performed mighty deeds with his arm;

He has scattered those who are proud in their inmost thoughts.

He has brought down rulers from their thrones but has lifted up the humble.

He has filled the hungry with good things but sent the rich away empty.

He has helped his servant Israel, remembering to be merciful to Abraham and his descendants forever, even as he said to our fathers" (Luke 1:46-55).

Mary stayed with Elizabeth for three months. Elizabeth was now up to her delivery time. The mentoring that must have taken place between the middle- aged woman and the young woman was invaluable. *Father, give unto me the heart of Elizabeth until I die.*

The heart of Elizabeth was able to recognize the tremendous gift God was giving the world through a young teenager. This same heart, imparted to her son, John, would be seen when he introduces Mary's son, the Messiah, to the world and he exclaims, "He must become greater; I must become less" (John 31:30). We do not read about Elizabeth again. Her son becomes a powerful preacher of repentance. What extravagant and amazing love!!

Upon arriving home Mary found God had groomed her Joseph to be her caretaker. There is no mention that God spoke directly to her again. He always spoke through her caretaker, Joseph. I have acquired great respect for the men in her life who released her to fulfill God's assignment. I desire her spirit that will say in every circumstance, "I am the Lord's servant. May it be to me as you have said."

Anna the Elderly

Anna was a widow for eighty-four years. We do not know how old she was when she was married but there is no doubt she was now in the hundred-year- old bracket. In Luke 2:36-38 we read this account: "There was also a prophetess, Anna, the daughter of Phanuel, of the tribe of Asher. She was very old; she had lived with her husband seven years after her marriage, and then was a widow until she was eighty-four. She never left the temple but worshipped night and day, fasting and praying. Coming up to them at that very moment, she gave thanks to God and spoke about the child to all who were looking forward to the redemption of Jerusalem." She was so in love with God that she immediately recognized the will and purposes of God in a little baby.

I was forty-three when an incredible assignment was given to me. Before that, my world was relatively safe and predictable. Through a neighborhood Bible study God began to enlarge my territory. He sent Elizabeths and Annas into my life who saw me moving beyond my limited territory. They believed in who I was and who God had called me to be and saw the giftings God had placed in my life. They were not jealous or envious, but drew out of me a song for the Lord. They taught, encouraged, and challenged me to look beyond myself and into the fields of the harvest. God used them to push me out of my comfortable nest of a predictable life into an adventurous journey. They said, "Fly Woman!" and I did. I am now seventy-five and I am still flying. I want to continue to love God with such a passion that to my last breath I will draw the purposes of God out of the young, middle-aged, and the elderly! To each I say: *This is now your hour!*

To the Young Women

Rise up, embrace your womanhood! Dare to give your past to Jesus. Let Him show you His plan and purposes for your life. Do not believe the lies of the enemy. May you have the spirit of Mary, who although she did not understand how it could happen, boldly said, "May it be to me as you have said." By faith knowing all things are possible with God.

Paul instructs young Timothy in 1 Timothy 5:12, to "Let no one despise your youth but be an example to the believers in word, in conduct, in love, in spirit, in faith and in purity."

Listen! If you obey God and do things God's way, God will take care of your Joseph. Never compromise God's principles of purity because of fear of losing your Joseph. The Joseph that God is grooming for you is one that will protect you and care for you. Make sure that he loves God and that together you draw out the assignments of God in each other.

Middle-Aged Women

Rise up! This is your hour! You have gained much wisdom. God has been preparing you for such a time as this. Do not let yourself become trapped with the world's thinking. Your usefulness is about to explode.

The world says you are going downhill and your beauty is fading, and therefore, so is your value. You feel that you have too many changes happening and regrets to be able to enjoy middle age. "Oh, if I would have only done this or if I would have only done that," you lament. The children are leaving the nest and you know you were not the perfect mother. Life hasn't been the fairy tale story you used to dream of; life has not been fair! The enemy is there to agree with you. "Life is over for you Baby, you got the wrinkles. Where did you get that stomach ledge?" And your husband is bombarded daily with all those beautiful figures on billboards, in magazine's, at shopping malls, and on television. Do not despair! Do not listen! These are lies from the enemy.

Our value is not in the way we look. The fashions of this world will not ever replace the beauty that radiates from a woman in love with Jesus. It is a temptation to become consumed with your regrets and the "what if's" and the "if only I had's" rather than seeing the opportunities to invest what we have learned through our mistakes and our successes in the next generation.

The older we get, the more dangerous we are to hell. We have seen God's faithfulness down through the years and every hard place we have walked through is a reminder again that life here is very short. As we keep walking as children of promise, we give hope to a lost world. We are leaving a legacy of life to future generations. The reason we are still here is to take as many people with us as possible. We are women of purpose. We know why we were born, what we are here for, and where we are going!

Elderly Women of God

Lift up your heads! This is no time to feel sorry for yourselves. The most powerful release of Jesus' ministry is through prayer. Jesus said we are to "pray the Lord of the harvest to send forth reapers." When we are no longer able to go, we can still be praying for those that are able. It is not a season we can afford to feel sorry for ourselves. To my last breath I want to draw songs out of the young, affirm the will and purposes of God in all the saints, and be in your cheering section as we head towards the finish line.

A few days ago we celebrated the life and memory of a precious young lady who was killed instantly in a car crash. We could celebrate because we knew where she was going on this last leg of her journey. The most important item on any of our daily agendas is to make ourselves ready for eternity and to pray for others to get ready also.

Just as we should not despise our youth, we should not allow the enemy to steal our middle and senior years through discouragement or depression. The ministry of Jesus never ends in our lives. I want Him to be so much a part of my life that even if I could not talk He would at least shine out of my eyeballs!

John had it right, "He must become greater; I must become less." That is the pathway to greatness, when you can actually get excited over the gifts in another and draw out of them what God has in them. So embrace the natural changes, do not grow weary, and continue to fight the good fight! We will finish the race and we will keep the faith, Amen!

CHAPTER 9

Warning:
Contents Under Pressure

*L*ight and *life* are two words used to describe Jesus. Isaiah prophesied in chapter nine that the people who were walking in darkness would see a great light. A light was going to dawn and it would shatter the yoke that was burdening them and the bar across their shoulder, which the oppressor had put on them, was going to be broken. A child, the son of God, Jesus, would be that light. The government would be upon His shoulders and he would be called wonderful, counselor, the mighty God, the everlasting Father, the Prince of Peace!

John said, "In Him was life, and that life was the light of men" (John 1:4). The struggle for the Christian is to remember to choose life. This life, this light, brings restoration, renewal, and revival to our darkened souls. "This is the verdict: Light has come into the world, but men loved darkness instead of light because their deeds were evil. Everyone who does evil hates the light, and will not come into the light for fear that his deeds will be exposed. But whoever lives by the truth comes into the light, so that it may be seen plainly that what he has done has been done through God." (John 3:19-21)

Eugene Peterson, in *the Message*, tells it to the world in this way in John 1:3-5: "Everything was created through him; nothing—not one thing!— came into being without him. What came into existence was Life, and the Life was Light to live by. The Life-Light blazed out of the darkness; the darkness couldn't put it out."

Satan could care less about us. He hates God and he knows that we are God's prized possessions. He attempts to undermine our confidence in Jesus. He will do anything to convince us God really does not love us and that God would never consider living within us. Listen to what Christ taught us: "You are the light of the world. A city on a hill cannot be hidden neither do people light a lamp and put it under a bowl. Instead they put it on a stand, and it gives light to everyone in the house. In the same way, let your light shine before men, that they may see your good deeds and praise your Father in heaven." (Matthew 5:14-16)

This is the secret of our victory. God's light in us lights up our lives and will light up the world. This is the process of regeneration, of restoration and revival. We allow God's truth to expose all darkness, and by way of repentance and confession, we continue to walk in life and light.

As Eugene Peterson writes, "The Word became flesh and blood, and moved into the neighborhood." And Satan does not like this new neighbor! Christ prepares us for this onslaught of hatred by teaching, "The thief comes only to steal and kill and destroy; I have come that they may have life, and have it to the full."

1 Timothy 6:6 tells us, "But godliness with contentment is great gain." A thief doesn't want our garbage, he wants our valuables, our wealth. The wealth that is found in the body of Christ is through His inhabitation of us. Does the devil walk right in and take these valuables? No! He finds our vulnerable areas. He will dress himself up as an angel of light and will agree with all of our wonderful sacrifices made for the Gospel. He waits until we are overworked, weary, and stressed out, and then throws in a hint that maybe we are being taken for granted and unappreciated.

Walking It Out

I was sitting in a large church of three thousand people waiting for the service to begin and replaying in my mind the previous couple of days' events. I had been at an International Aglow board meeting where there had been much discussion over some needed changes and I had left the meeting extremely frustrated. I had not understood a lot of what was being said and I had been too proud to expose my ignorance to the entire group. Later that night, when I returned to my room, the Lord reminded me that I had been asking Him to teach me how to walk in the spirit and not in the flesh. Immediately I knew He was asking me to bring this frustration before the others and into the light by confessing my ignorance to the entire group. I did not want to do it, I even told God I would rather go to the whipping post.

The next morning, after I shared my heart with the group, others began to express that they too had some of the same concerns and questions. Once it was out in the open and in the light we could work together to get the answers to our questions. If I had not been obedient and brought to light my frustrations, I could have done great damage to this ministry.

As I continued to wait for the service to start, I felt the Lord say, "You have been asking me to teach you about humility. I have brought you here this morning to show you a living example." A man who served as a deacon at the church was going to give the morning message. I was a bit disappointed, as I had been looking forward to hearing the senior pastor. His text was 1 Timothy 6:6 and John 10:10. As he began to speak he shared three areas the enemy uses to steal our contentment.

First: Who we are. He will belittle, intimidate, and put you down. He will try to get us dissatisfied with ourselves. We are not to compare ourselves with others by wishing we could be like someone else. There can be only one of us. If we try to be who we are not, we are in essence telling God we are not willing to be uniquely ourselves, whom He, Himself created.

Second: What we do: Comparing our positions, education, and jobs. He will make you feel that your job or assignment is insignificant. Mothers quite often fall prey to this attack. "You are living in Dullsville. You need to be on the cutting edge! You are not appreciated." Or, "What kind of mother would leave her child at day care all day!"

Our children battle this daily. Those who are gifted academically or in sports get more attention than those who are not. Those children probably work just as hard for their C's and sports abilities as the others and receive no recognition.

Third: What we have: Comparing our homes, furnishings, cars, clothing, spouses, children, and so forth. Prosperity can put the emphasis on the wrong things.

Warning Signs

Anger, unthankfulness, murmuring, complaining, faultfinding and being easily offended are early warning signs of degeneration. If not confessed and repented of, these will produce resentment, bitterness, and slander, and with these you will begin to filter everything you hear. You become the prosecuting attorney, judge, and jury. You can no longer look at the facts objectively.

"See to it that no one misses the grace of God and that no bitter root grows up to cause trouble and defile many." Hebrews 12:15

This man began to share how as a deacon he felt he was less important than the rest of the leadership. His title wasn't as impressive as pastor or elder. A leadership meeting was scheduled and he assumed he was to be there, only to have someone ask him why he had come. That confirmed it. He was not as important as the other leadership.

He went home and shared this with his wife. He also shared this with his friends and the more he talked about it the more it consumed him. His friends began to carry this offense and unknown to the leadership this group was getting ready to leave the church.

His wife, being a very discerning woman, made a reservation at a motel for him and suggested he get by himself and pray until he heard from God. When he saw what he had done he wept. He went home and gathered his family together and confessed his sin. He went to his friends and again repentance and forgiveness flowed. He then went to the leadership and such healing took place that the senior pastor asked if he would share it with the church body.

I could personally relate to the insecurities that had driven this man to compare himself to others. I myself had often been a sounding board for hurting people and had taken on their offenses. I realized that the moment we take on the offenses of others we disqualify ourselves from being part of the solution and can make the problem more complicated and deadly.

It starts with discontentment but soon will consume your thought life. Next it will lead you to faulty thinking, which then produces wrong conclusions and which will lead you to wrong attitudes and judgments. The deacon gave five steps to stop this process and get us back to a heart of repentance: (1) Recognize it; (2) Confess it; (3) Repent of it; (4) Make restitution; and (5) Return to Godliness and contentment and keep on walking.

At the closing of the service he gave an opportunity for anyone who was caught in similar circumstances to come to the altar. I had expected a few would respond but the altar and aisles were full as people streamed forward and exposed the darkness that was in their own lives.

Paul wrote in Philippians 4:11-13 that "...for I have learned to be content whatever the circumstances. I know what it is to be in need, and I know what is is to have plenty. I have learned the secret of being content in any and every situation, whether well fed or hungry, whether living in plenty or want. I can do everything through him who gives me strength."

"Keep your lives free from the love of money and be content with what you have, because God has said, 'Never will I leave you; never will I forsake you.'" (Hebrews 13:5-6)

Snare of the Fowler

I returned from a trip to China and I had not slept much for three days. I was emotionally and physically depleted. One evening a few days later, I went to our midweek prayer time. A precious brother walked up to me and said, "I don't pray for you, I pray for your husband." He was concerned for some health problems Wallace was experiencing. I was glad he was covering my husband in prayer but on this particular evening what he said hurt me deeply.

A few days later one of our elders was at our home and said something that I took as sharp and cutting. I knew this man well and our relationship was usually very open, but fatigue can cause us to hear a distorted message. I did what I teach other women to do. I went past my feelings and down into my spirit and said, "Father, I know that these men did not mean to hurt me and I do forgive them."

But later on I found myself avoiding them. I knew that I had forgiven them but I had lost my freedom to be myself. The enemy had found a weakness: I did not want to be hurt again. I knew I could not afford to give the enemy any leverage, or my fellowship with other believers would be ruined.

I went to prayer meeting that week and I purposely sat behind the first brother. Before he could get away, I tapped him on the shoulder and said, "I know you are a man of God and I know you never meant to hurt me. There is a dark thing that is trying to hide in me. But if you will allow me to expose this, I know it will be gone."

I shared with him the incident, then he said, "What a terrible thing to have said." I said, "I have done the same thing many times." The Bible calls them idle words. As soon as it was exposed, it was gone!

The next Sunday after church, I went to our elder. He could not even remember saying anything like that but said that his wife had been telling him he could sound cutting sometimes. We now laugh about the incident and have learned it is very important not to allow darkness a hiding place.

The River

"On the last day, that great day of the feast, Jesus stood and cried out, saying, 'If anyone thirsts, let him come to Me and drink. He who believes in Me, as the Scripture has said, out of his heart will flow rivers of living water.' But this He spoke concerning the Spirit, whom those believing in Him would receive;" (John 7:37-39a)

The Bible warns us we are to guard our hearts for the heart is the well spring of life. Whoever and whatever touches the river, experiences life! Hell's one great fear is of the river. If Satan can convince us we are justified to carry offenses and self pity, unforgiveness and anger, malice and worry, fear and frustrations, gossip and slander, these will create log jams in the river and will stop the flow. The enemy knows that if the church really believes that this river is in her, she will devastate the kingdom of darkness.

Absalom and Tamar

Absalom and Amnon were both King David's sons but from different wives. Absalom had a beautiful sister named Tamar and Amnon was in love with her. One day Amnon's friend, whom the Bible describes as a shrewd man, came up with a plan. Upon his advice, Amnon pretended he was ill and asked his father to send Tamar to his house so she could prepare him a meal.

King David sent her over and when she brought the food to him he raped her. She begged him not to and was even willing to marry him but he wouldn't listen to her. Afterwards when he was through with her, he hated her and sent her out of his house in utter disgrace.

Absalom took *her* into his house and the *offense* into his heart. We read later that he pretended as though everything was all right. It sounded as though he was doing her a kindness, but when he took the offense into his heart he disqualified himself from ever being an answer.

"See to it that no one misses the grace of God and that no bitter root grows up to cause trouble and defile many."

When King David heard what happened he was very angry but he did nothing about it. For two years the pressure of Absalom's anger built until it erupted into full blown bitterness. Absalom killed Amnon and then he fled into exile for three more years.

Joab tricked David into letting Absalom come home but David would not see or talk to him. Two more years passed before he saw or talked to his son. By this time Absalom, in his hatred, had begun to formulate his revenge into a plan to destroy his father.

One man caught my attention as I was reading this story. I wanted to know more about Ahithophel. He was David's trusted counselor. Second Samuel 16:23 describes him: "Now in those days the advice Ahithophel gave was like that of one who inquires of God." I wanted to know why he went over on Absalom's side. I discovered he was Bathsheba's grandfather. It could well be he had never forgiven David for getting Bathsheba pregnant and then killing her husband Uriah by putting him on the front line of battle. Could he have been carrying unforgiveness all those years?

He advised Absalom to lie with his father's concubines that were left behind when David fled. As I pointed out earlier, Ahithophel was Bathsheba's grandfather and I found it very interesting that he advised Absalom to commit the same type of sexual sin that David had committed with Bathsheba.

Later, when Absalom did not follow his advice concerning the battle plan, Ahithophel saddled his donkey, went home, set his house in order, and hung himself. If it is a man of God who allows unresolved anger to turn into bitterness, it will eventually work its way out in one way or another. In this case he eventually took his own life.

The armies of Israel were defeated by David's men. Twenty thousand lost their lives that day because they followed the cause of one man who allowed an offense to hide in his heart. As I read this I could not help but think of the devastation and sorrow this must have brought to twenty thousand families and their friends back home. Our choices will affect lives for eternity. If we choose life we bring life to others around us; if we choose death, we bring death to those around us. We have a fresh reminder in our own nation. When we look at all the men, women, and children who were affected here in America by the bitterness of a few men on September 11, 2001.

Deuteronomy 30:19,20 says, "This day I call heaven and earth as witnesses against you that I have set before you life and death, blessings and curses. Now choose life, so that you and your children may live and that you may love the Lord your God, listen to his voice, and hold fast to him. For the Lord is your life, and he will give you many years in the land he swore to give to your fathers, Abraham, Isaac and Jacob."

Our choices affect the people around us. No man lives or dies unto himself. If one man's bad choice could take twenty thousand with him to their deaths, plus affect all who were left behind, then surely a right choice for life is more powerful. Wouldn't you like to influence at least twenty thousand people for life before you die?

"See to it that no one misses the grace of God and that no bitter root grows up to cause trouble and defile many." (Hebrew 12: 15)

CHAPTER 10

Traveling Hazards

"This day I call heaven and earth as witnesses against you
that I have set before you life and death, blessings and curses.
Now choose life, so that you and your children may live."
Deuteronomy 30:19

It is my firm belief that there is no deeper teaching than the love
walk. We talk about deeper teaching and yet we cannot get along
with each other. The Bible warns us against discord and division,
time and again. Paul admonished the Corinthian church in 1
Corinthians chapter 3. The Corinthians were comparing themselves
by the men they followed. Some said they were followers of Paul
and others of Apollos. They failed to comprehend they were a part
of one body, the body of Christ and that where one may plant,
another may water, and another harvest that which was planted for
the gospel.

A chain can be used to illustrate this concept. There are many
links that make up a chain. If it were just one solid link there would
be no flexibility and no way to add to the length and it would be
limited in its use. In the design of the links there is flexibility and
the potential for added length so that the chain can extend farther.

Then we must consider the metal itself. If the process for

tempering the steel is not watched diligently, or the metals are blended incorrectly, the link will be weak and may break under stress. Everyone in the body of Christ, the Church, is essential to the length and strength of this chain. We can never be the whole chain in anyone's life. There are many people God uses to set one person free. Understand this, Church! We are not just to be pew sitters. If our link weakens due to our lack of attention, the chain will break and the Church will not be able to accomplish its assignment.

Paul writes to us that there is only one foundation and that is Jesus Christ but we must be careful of how we build. If we only build our lives by wood, hay, and stubble, all we have built will perish. Anything that comes from the flesh, apart from the Spirit of God, will be burned up. Take for example the writing of this book. If I am just writing it to prove I can write a book, or to make a name for myself, it will be worthless. "If any man builds on this foundation using gold, silver, costly stones, wood, hay or straw, his work will be shown for what it is, because the Day will bring it to light. It will be revealed with fire, and the fire will test the quality of each man's work. If what he has built survives, he will receive his reward. If it is burned up, he will suffer loss; he himself will be saved, but only as one escaping through the flames." (1 Corinthians 3:12-15) But, if I am writing this book to tell the truths that I have learned in order to strengthen the body of Christ then it will become as precious stones and be of value to all who read its pages.

I am not writing this book to gain God's favor; I already have that. We do not have to earn God's friendship it is always there for us. It is often our own insecurities that keep us from this friendship. My children do not have to earn the right to be my children they are my children. I would love them if they went out and robbed a bank. Whenever they give me gifts it is not to earn my favor. It is to express their appreciation and love for me being their mother.

When I make breakfast for my family, do I go out and make the breakfast because I have to? No, I go out to the kitchen because I want to bless my husband and family. I don't have to earn their love; I have it. I just want to bless them and show them my love and that I value them. The flesh always will tell us, "You have to do this." The spirit will say, "No, I get to do this."

How sad it would be to stand before Jesus and hear him say, "It wasn't my ministry you were doing. You were just working for Me, but not doing My work. Yes, people were saved, churches were started, miracles happened, counseling was provided, but you were trying to earn your way, you were doing it for your glory and not Mine." In our flesh we are paupers. "Don't you know that you yourselves are God's temple and that God's Spirit lives in you? If anyone destroys God's temple, God will destroy him; for God's temple is sacred, and you are that temple."

The fruit of his residence in us is love, joy, peace, patience, kindness, goodness, faithfulness, gentleness, and self-control. We have everything that we are ever going to need to live out this Christian life. The gifts of the Holy Spirit are not ours to keep. They are to give away. I like how Eugene Peterson describes it: "You realize, don't you, that you are the temple of God, and God himself is present in you? No one will get by with vandalizing God's temple, you can be sure of that. God's temple is sacred— and you, remember, *are* the temple."

I admire the way that Eugene Peterson can capture the truth and pen it into everyday language. In Romans 12:3-6 he translates it like this: "The only accurate way to understand ourselves is by what God is and by what he does for us, not by what we are and what we do for him.

In this way we are like the various parts of a human body. Each part gets its meaning from the body as a whole, not the other way around. The body we're talking about is Christ body of chosen people. Each of us finds our meaning and function as a part of His body. But as a chopped-off finger or a cut-off toe we wouldn't amount to much, would we? So since we find ourselves fashioned into all these excellently formed and marvelously functioning parts in Christ's body, let's just go ahead and be what we were made to be, without enviously or pridefully comparing ourselves with each other, or trying to be something we aren't."

King Asa

In the fall of 1993, I had a lot of questions. Why were ministries

falling and why were they struggling financially? It seemed everywhere I looked God's soldiers were weary. The divorce rate was
increasing in the church, our Aglow chapters were closing faster
than new ones were being formed, and strife, competition, and divi-
sions were increasing in the church. Why?

Second Chronicles 14-16 tells one of the saddest stories in
history. King Asa was King Solomon's grandson. Asa started out as
a good king and he did what was good in the eyes of the Lord his
God. He brought great reforms in his day and he commanded Judah
to seek the Lord, the God of their fathers, and to obey His
commands. He removed the foreign altars and high places, and he
had the sacred stones smashed, the asherah poles cut down, and the
high places and incense altars removed in every town. Judah was at
peace under him. He built up the fortified cities and put walls
around them with towers, gates, and bars.

True humility is remembering who God is and who we are in
Him and allowing Him to live His life in us. He loves to prosper the
truly humble, obedient, and faithful child of God. Asa had an army
of 300,000 men. One day Zerah the Cushite marched against him
with an army more than twice as big. What does a humble man do?
He calls to the Lord his God and says, "Lord, there is no one like
you to help the powerless against the mighty. Help us, O Lord our
God, for we rely on you, and in your name we have come against
this vast army. O Lord, you are our God; do not let man prevail
against you."

God heard the cry of a humble man and gave them a glorious
victory. "This is the one I esteem: he who is humble and contrite in
spirit, and trembles at my word" (Isaiah 66:2). "Humble yourselves
before the Lord, and he will lift you up" (James 4:10). "He mocks
proud mockers but gives grace to the humble." (Proverbs 3:34).
God had said to King Solomon, Asa's grandfather, "If my people,
who are called by my name, will humble themselves and pray and
seek my face and turn from their wicked ways, then will I hear from
heaven and will forgive their sin and will heal their land" (2
Chronicles 7:14).

In chapter 15 God sent Azariah to meet King Asa and when he
met him he said, "Listen to me, Asa and all Judah and Benjamin.

The Lord is with you when you are with him. If you seek him, he will be found by you, but if you forsake him, he will forsake you" (2 Chronicles 15:2).

No Longer Humble

But something happened to King Asa during his years of prosperity. When he was a humble man the anointing was so heavily on him that large numbers came from the land of Israel just to live under his reign. They saw the Lord was with him and he brought about wonderful reforms. They entered into a covenant to seek the Lord, the God of their fathers, with all their heart and soul. So the Lord gave them rest on every side. There was no more war until the thirty-fifth year of his reign. Chapter 16 then describes his last years.

In the thirty-sixth year of Asa's reign, King Baasha of Israel went up against Judah and fortified Ramah to prevent anyone from leaving or entering the territory of King Asa of Judah. But this time Asa no longer sought the face of God, but went to a heathen king for help. How could he do such a thing? Why? Because he was no longer a humble man.

Pride takes the credit for your accomplishments instead of giving God the glory. God in His mercy sent Hanani, the seer to Asa and in 2 Chronicles 16:7,8 it reads, "At that time Hanani the seer came to Asa king of Judah and said to him, 'Because you relied on the king of Aram and not on the Lord your God, the army of the King of Aram has escaped from your hand. Were not the Cushites and Libyans a mighty army with great numbers of chariots and horsemen? Yet when you relied on the Lord, he delivered them into your hand.'" Verse 9 here is very significant. "For the eyes of the Lord range throughout the earth to strengthen those whose hearts are fully committed to him. You have done a foolish thing, and from now on you will be at war."

Asa became so enraged with the seer that he put him into prison. At the same time Asa brutally oppressed some of the people. I am sure this sad story was recorded to prevent the same tragedy from happening in our own lives. He started out so well and ended up so wrong. He was later afflicted with a disease of his feet and even though it was severe he still did not seek help from the Lord but only from his doctors.

In verses 13-14 we see his end: "Then in the forty-first year of his reign Asa died and rested with his fathers. They buried him in the tomb that he had cut out for himself in the City of David. They laid him on a bier covered with spices and various blended perfumes, and they made a huge fire in his honor."

Pride is the product of the flesh and the flesh is an enemy of the cross. "Pride goes before destruction, and a haughty spirit before a fall" (Proverbs 16:18). Isn't it interesting that Asa would be struck down in his feet, his physical foundation? His feet were literally taken out from under him. When Asa began he was teachable and trusting, but somewhere he replaced his godly foundation with himself and began to take the credit for his success. You would have thought that he would have learned something from what happened to King Saul.

Self-Promotion and Self-Importance

In Samuel 15:1-3 we read how God instructed Saul through Samuel to destroy all that belonged to the Amalekites because they had caused the Israelites trouble as they came out of Egypt. Saul disobeyed and spared Agag, the king, and also the best of the sheep and cattle of the flock. When Samuel confronted Saul he blamed it on the soldiers and also dared to say that he brought the best of the flock so the people could sacrifice to the Lord.

The Lord gave a message to Saul through Samuel: "Although you were once small in your own eyes, did you not become the head of the tribes of Israel? The Lord anointed you king over Israel. And He sent you on a mission, saying, 'Go and completely destroy those wicked people, the Amalekites; make war on them until you have wiped them out.' Why did you not obey the Lord? Why did you pounce on the plunder and do evil in the eyes of the Lord?"

"'But I did obey the Lord,' Saul said. 'I went on the mission the Lord assigned me. I completely destroyed the Amalekites and brought back Agag their king. The soldiers took sheep and cattle from the plunder, the best of what was devoted to God, in order to sacrifice them to the Lord your God at Gilgal'" (1 Samuel 15:17-21).

I find that very sad when he said "your God." He could no longer say "my God." When the arm of flesh replaces the hand of God there are many casualties.

Samuel's words to Saul are a reminder to us, what is important to God and also what grieves Him. "Does the Lord delight in burnt offerings and sacrifices as much as in obeying the voice of the Lord? To obey is better then sacrifice, and to heed is better than the fat of rams. For rebellion is like the sin of divination, and arrogance like the evil of idolatry. Because you have rejected the word of the Lord, he has rejected you as king"(1 Samuel 15:22,23).

Self-importance and self-promotion are the result of pride. It leads to arrogance, self-centeredness, conceit, and deception. Jesus warned in Matthew 7:15-23: "Watch out for false prophets. They come to you in sheep's clothing, but inwardly they are ferocious wolves. By their fruit you will recognize them. Do people pick grapes from thorn bushes, or figs from thistles? Likewise every good tree bears good fruit, but a bad tree bears bad fruit. A good tree cannot bear bad fruit, and a bad tree cannot bear good fruit. Every tree that does not bear good fruit is cut down and thrown into the fire. Thus, by their fruit you will recognize them... "Many will say to me on that day, 'Lord, Lord, did we not prophesy in your name, and in your name drive out demons and perform many miracles?' Then I will tell them plainly, 'I never knew you. Away from me, you evildoers!'"

The greater the revelation of who I am in Christ Jesus the more I am excited about His ministry in you and me. We surrender our bodies along with our unique personalities. I know I am not everybody's favorite speaker. I often tell people, "Don't worry about that, someone else will draw out of you the purposes of God!" As His story is told through each of our unique personalities it keeps the Word of God fresh. The more I understand this truth the more I will appreciate His ministry in you. Even as I write this book, it will surely have a distinct tone that can be recognized as only my unique way of expression.

Jesus, in Matthew 24 and 25, answered the question of what to watch out for as we move towards the end of time. Even though no man knows the day and the hour, He does say when you see certain things happening on the earth, we are to "Stand up and lift up your heads, because your redemption is drawing near." We are to be on the alert and not allow the thief to break into our houses. He describes a faithful servant who his master put in charge of his house while he went on a journey. He was to give his servants all they needed until he came back. He said that the servant will truly be blessed if the master finds that he was faithful when he returned. But if the servant wasn't faithful and began to mistreat his fellow servants, the master would cut him to pieces and assign him a place with the hypocrites, where there will be weeping, and gnashing of teeth.

Jesus tells the story of the ten virgins who took their lamps and went out to meet the bridegroom. Five were wise and five were foolish. The five wise took oil with them but the five foolish did not. While they were waiting for Him to come the foolish had used up their oil supply. At midnight the cry went out that He was coming and they quickly asked for the wise to share some of their oil with them. But the wise ones advised the foolish to go to those who sold oil and buy their own. While they were on the way, the bridegroom came and they did not make it to the wedding supper. They begged for Him to open the door but the Bridegroom answered, "I tell you the truth, I don't know you."

Salvation is free but the anointing will cost you your life in exchange for His. May I say it another way, it will cost you your ministry in exchange for His. I do not want to be working for Jesus when He comes; I want to be doing His works. There is a big difference! One is the energy of the flesh and the other is the life of God flowing through us working out the life of God in us. For years I was working for Him instead of letting Him work through me. I am still in process but I find Him ever faithful and I never want Him to let me get away with anything.

In Matthew 25 we read the story of the talents. The story starts with a man going on a journey. He called his servants and gave five talents to one, two talents to another, and one talent to a third. When he returned he called them together again to see what they had done with the giftings he had entrusted to them.

The first servant doubled his talents and the master was very pleased. The second servant accomplished the same and again the master was pleased. The third reported that he was afraid of the master and knew him to be a hard man so he buried his one talent and when the master returned he gave him back what he had been given. The master was not happy with this servant and the judgment on him was very harsh. He called him worthless and threw him outside into the darkness where there is weeping and gnashing of teeth.

I found it interesting that the third servant had already decided before he received the talent what he was going to do with it. When he remarks, "I knew that you are a hard man, harvesting where you have not sown and gathering where you have not scattered seed", he already had formed a rebellious attitude towards the master. He was not going to bother using his "gifting" because he did not want to.

That is why it is so dangerous to bury His gifting in us: it is not ours. It is for the benefit of the body. If you bury it and are not faithful with using it to benefit the body, God will remove it and give it to someone else who will be faithful and obedient.

As we have looked at King Asa and King Saul and heard the warnings of Jesus, we see obedience that comes from a humble heart and a love for God, will not go wrong.

I close the chapter with Paul's words in 1 Corinthians 13 as paraphrased by Eugene Peterson:

"If I speak with human eloquence and angelic ecstasy but don't love, I'm nothing but the creaking of a rusty gate.

If I speak God's Word with power, revealing all his mysteries and making everything plain as day, and if I have faith that says to a mountain, "Jump," and it jumps, but I don't love, I'm nothing.

If I give everything I own to the poor and even go to the stake to be burned as a martyr, but I don't love, I've gotten nowhere. So, no matter what I say, what I believe, and what I do, I'm bankrupt without love.

Love never gives up.

Love cares more for others than for self.

Love doesn't want what it doesn't have.

Love doesn't strut,

Doesn't have a swelled head,

Doesn't force itself on others,

Isn't always "me first,"
Doesn't fly off the handle,
Doesn't keep score of the sins of others,
Doesn't revel when others grovel,
Takes pleasure in the flowering of truth,
Puts up with anything,
Trusts God always,
Always looks for the best,
Never looks back,
But keeps going to the end.

Love never dies. Inspired speech will be over some day; praying in tongues will end; understanding will reach its limit. We know only a portion of the truth, and what we say about God is always incomplete. But when the Complete arrives, our incompletes will be canceled.

When I was an infant at my mother's breast, I gurgled and cooed like any infant. When I grew up, I left those infant ways for good.

We don't yet see things clearly. We're squinting in a fog, peering through a mist. But it won't be long before the weather clears and the sun shines bright! We'll see it all then; see it all as clearly as God sees us, knowing him directly just as he knows us!

But for right now, until that completeness, we have three things to do to lead us toward that consummation: Trust steadily in God, hope unswervingly, love extravagantly. And the best of the three is love."

CHAPTER 11

The Final Destination

"**L**adies and Gentlemen, please make sure your seat belts are securely fastened and your tables and seat backs are in an upright and locked position. We are only a breath away from the great city, the New Jerusalem."

We are at last approaching the final descent of this journey. The journey at times has been very turbulent and we are eager to be released from these cramped and restricted confines and long to be able to stretch. I have wondered what discomforts Paul must have endured as he sat writing in prison. Yet, he confidently knew why he was there and where he was going, never losing sight of his purpose and final destination. That is why he could write "for me to live is Christ, to die is gain." Oh, to remain faithful and focused to the end like men like Todd Beamer who, knowing he would probably die on Flight 93 that fateful day, September 11th, chose to save as many people as possible. Only God knows just how many were saved by the bravery of those men who rushed into that cockpit. "For me to live is Christ, to die is gain."

Second Timothy was Paul's last letter and it is believed he wrote it just before his execution. As you read his letter you can sense Paul's urgency. He had mentored Timothy, as a spiritual son, and was now passing him the baton as he urged him to keep his focus in the midst of strong persecution. As you read this letter you can feel his heart for this young man: "You therefore my son, be strong in the grace that is in Christ Jesus and the things you have heard from me among many witnesses, commit to faithful men who will be able to teach others also. You therefore must endure hardship as a good soldier of Christ Jesus." (2 Timothy 2:1-2 AMP)

"For I already am being poured out as a drink offering, and the time of my departure is at hand. *I have fought the good fight, I have finished the race, I have kept the faith, henceforth there is laid up for me a crown of righteousness, which the Lord the righteous Judge will grant me in that day and not to me only but to all those who love His appearing.*"

It is so freeing to know our times are in His hands. I pray that my life will be a living testimony of His wonderful love and grace. I have often declared that I shall live out my allotted days and will not go home until it is His time and in His time only. In the meantime, I will live under His Lordship. He is the driver, pilot, engineer and whatever other name you want to call the person in charge.

At seventy-five, I see changes in this earthly body of mine. The enemy would love to tell me my value is diminishing and that I soon will be in the way of the young, instead of a blessing to them. I am enjoying this time of my life and all the benefits that come with it, like being able to relate to my children and grandchildren as adults, looking forward to my social security check every month, and enjoying all the senior citizen discounts. There is the joy of watching my children and grandchildren make right choices, choose their mates carefully, and above all else, love the Lord. I have stood on the promises in the Word of God and have attempted to pass this on to the next generation. Now I am seeing His Word come to pass: "As for me, this is my covenant with them," says the Lord. "My Spirit, who is on you, and my words that I have put in your mouth will not depart from your mouth, or from the mouths of your children, or from the mouths of their descendants from this time on and forever," says the Lord.

Wallace and I will have been married fifty-five years. As older people we have experienced God's grace and faithfulness. We know much more now about the power of prayer and how to be prayer *warriors* instead of worriers. With this new understanding we can better pray for the coming generations as they get ready to receive the baton of the future.

There are also new and challenging hurdles we face as we age. The thought of losing our independence and the inability to do things for ourselves is disturbing. A few years ago I dislocated my shoulder and this gave me a taste of what it would be like needing help, to dress, cut my meat, basically to care for myself. I didn't like it very much.

We have accumulated much wisdom through trial and error along the way. We want to shield our children and grandchildren from the pain of wrong choices. But we need to allow them to learn from their failures just as we did. We must not grow critical of their lives and we may have to pray and support them in endeavors we are not certain of.

The mother eagle acts uncaring as she pulls out the feathers and the fur from the nest. When the eaglet is perched on the edge, she will even give it a push so the little one is forced to use its wings. But she is ever ready to swoop down under the fledgling and catch the falling eaglet, repeating this process until it can fly on its own. I see intercessory prayer as this swooping down and catching the fledglings who are learning to fly. Blessed is the child who has this kind of prayer covering.

I knew a gentleman who was so in love with God that even though he was in a nursing home needing total care, he would ask the nurses if he could pray for them first before they cared for his needs. While there he suffered a stroke and the nurses cried for fear he would die. He had touched their lives that much. His outer man may have been growing weaker but his inner man was gaining strength. His daughter would tell us stories of how he would look for ways to bless people. He continually prayed for our church and one Sunday morning his daughter, Marsha, brought him to the service. I can still see him, in my mind's eye, dressed in his navy blue striped suit and red tie, sitting in his wheel chair, radiant with the love of God. We gathered around him and prayed for him. With tears in my eyes I said, "Oh Brother, I want to love God like you do."

Will Your Anchor Hold?

As I have already said, prayer is the greatest way to release the ministry of Jesus. It can be released in wheel chairs, hospital beds, nursing homes, and in any other situation. We dare not waste time feeling sorry for ourselves. We have learned so much about the power in prayer, and we must use it.

I believe I shall see all my family around the throne. I love to remind God of His covenant promise that He made with us in Isaiah 59:21: "As for me, this is my covenant with them," says the Lord. "'My Spirit, who is on you, and my words that I have put in your mouth will not depart from your mouth, or from the mouths of your children, or from the mouths of their descendants from this time on and forever,' says the Lord."

I was speaking at a retreat in Dutchess, Alberta, Canada the weekend before September 11, 2001. Before I closed the weekend with 2 Timothy 3:1-5, I remarked that it was like reading one our newspapers today, or listening to the evening news. "But mark this: There will be terrible times in the last days. People will be lovers of themselves, lovers of money, boastful, proud, abusive, disobedient to their parents, ungrateful, unholy, without love, unforgiving, slanderous, without self-control, brutal, not lovers of the good, treacherous, rash, conceited, lovers of pleasure rather than lovers of God—having a form of godliness but denying its power. Have nothing to do with them."

God met us that night in a very special way. People responded with repentance to the Word of God and allowed the Holy Spirit to locate them.

At 2:00 am the next morning September the tenth, I awoke from a dream so horrendous that I spent the rest of the night praying. In the dream I saw people running and screaming with a big black cloud behind them. Fear and panic was on their faces as they searched for loved ones. I prayed God would give me the meaning of this dream. If this was just one of the enemy's scare tactics, I wanted to know, but I felt it was a warning of a terrible disaster about to take place.

The next morning, as we watched the planes crash into the

World Trade Center, I understood the dream. All of us, without a doubt, will never forget where we were when this manmade disaster happened.

This horrendous event has changed the way we think and relate with each other. It is a stark reminder that life is but a vapor, here one day and gone the next. This was, without a doubt, the most life-changing event in my time. I had experienced wars that were fought on foreign soil, but never on our homeland.

This present generation has embraced a false concept of security and now this is being shaken. We are not financially secure these days. Those of us who are counting heavily on the monthly social security checks for retirement are seeing that this could be gone overnight. Is it any wonder the Bible says that men's hearts will fail them because of fear when they see these things come to pass on the earth!

I can relate to Paul when he writes, "...for I have learned to be content whatever the circumstances. I know what it is to be in need, and I know what it is to have plenty. I have learned the secret of being content in any and every situation, whether will fed or hungry, whether living in plenty or in want. I can do everything through him who gives me strength."

Unless we are anchored to the Rock that cannot be moved, fear will control us. This will not only cause a shipwreck in our lives, but will also render us useless in helping the people around us.

Prosperity has in some ways been hard on the home, church, and the nation. Prosperity in itself is not bad but it can be a temptation to compromise and fit in with the dictates of the world. Having too much of anything makes life complicated, brings confusion and fosters ingratitude.

Sometimes I look back with nostalgia at the simple life I knew as a child. There were definitely some advantages in how we grew up. One such advantage was the joy of relaxation. It just seemed like we had more time. The pace of life wasn't so demanding. We enjoyed our evenings together, reading, singing, listening to the adults as they discussed politics or the Bible or whatever was news. Of course, God is the same whether we have little or whether we have much. As you enjoy your prosperity, remember to be thankful and not to abuse it. "To whom much has been given, much is required." And if you find yourself in prison for your faith, just remember Paul's words to young Timothy as he awaited the outcome of his prison term:

"But you keep your head in all situations, endure hardship, do the work of an evangelist, discharge all the duties of your ministry.

For I am already being poured out like a drink offering, and the time has come for my departure. I have fought the good fight, I have finished the race, I have kept the faith. Now there is in store for me the crown of righteousness, which the Lord, the righteous Judge, will award to me on that day—and not only to me, but also to all who have longed for his appearing" (2 Timothy 4:5-8).

Final Approach

"Ladies and Gentlemen, please make sure your seat belts are securely fastened and your tables and seat backs are in an upright and locked position as we are on our final approach to the Great City. You are only a breath away from the New Jerusalem! There will be a great reception prepared just for you and all those who accepted the invitation to be the Bride of the Son of God at the Marriage Supper of the Lamb.

By the way, there is no baggage claim here. The King Himself has provided all the wedding garments. All that is required is your identification and that has been written on you by the Father himself. (Rev. 3:12)

Enter in, and experience the fullness of joy you have so longed for. The journey has been long, but you have all eternity to rest in His presence!!"

"Then I heard what sounded like a great multitude, like the roar of rushing waters and like loud peals of thunder, shouting:

"Hallelujah!
For our Lord God Almighty reigns.
Let us rejoice and be glad
And give him glory!
For the wedding of the Lamb has come,

and his bride has made herself ready.
Fine linen, bright and clean,
was given her to wear."
(Fine linen stands for the righteous acts of the
    saints.)
Then the angel said to me, "Write: Blessed are those
    who are invited to the wedding supper of the
    Lamb!
And he added, "These are the true words of God."

Revelations 19:6-9

Printed in the United States
1288500005B/118-510